Foreword by Dr. Hutz Hertzberg

ADEQUATE!

How GOD Empowers Ordinary People to Serve

Bill Mills

Connecting With God for Growth and Ministries Series

These devotional Bible studies will help you grow in your relationship with the Lord and in your ministry.

Adequate! How God Empowers Ordinary People to Serve
(Also available in Chinese & Portuguese)
by Bill Mills

Language of the Heart: Knowing Joy and Communion in Prayer
by Bill Mills

Finishing Well in Life and Ministry:
God's Protection from Burnout
(Also available in Spanish and Chinese)
by Bill Mills and Craig Parro

Unlikely Warriors: Our Call to Invade the Darkness
by Craig Parro

Inductive Bible Study Series

These Bible study helps will enable you to grow in your understanding of the Scriptures and in your preparation for teaching.

Proverbs: Lessons for the Growing Years (for Jr/Sr High)

Jonah: Inductive Bible Study

Philippians: A Family Bible Study

Ruth: The Romance of Redemption

Inductive Bible Study Handbook
by Dennis Fledderjohann

A Servant Series

Each book contains 21 articles from many well-known authors. Great library resources!

Marriage, Parenting & Forgiveness
Reconciliation, Fellowship & the Grace of God

You may order our books and
Bible conference CDs on our web site:
www.LeadershipResources.org

Sixteenth Printing—2013

THIS MINISTRY IS DEDICATED TO

The Glory of God
The Honor of His Word
The Building Up of the Body of Christ

Such is the confidence that we have through Christ toward God. Not that we are sufficient in ourselves to claim anything as coming from us, but our sufficiency is from God, who has made us competent to be ministers of a new covenant, not of the letter but of the Spirit. For the letter kills, but the Spirit gives life.

2 Corinthians 3:4-6

Table of Contents

Foreword

T here is no greater joy, fulfillment, or satisfaction available to a human being this side of eternity than to serve in ministry as a pastor, missionary, or Christian lay leader. At the same time, no other calling can be as demanding, wearisome, and discouraging.

In my former role as Dean of Chapel at Trinity Evangelical Divinity School, I had the wonderful privilege of helping to prepare men and women for ministry in general, especially pastoral ministry. I am often encouraged by our students' desire for such service as they look forward to the future. However, I am also at times concerned as I see some equate completion of a rigorous academic program and the attainment of a divinity degree as all that is necessary to ensure a successful ministry. Now as I serve at Moody Church, we face similar challenges as we prepare God's servants for ministry.

These days, something more than a quality education, honed ministry skills, and strategic church placement is needed to sustain a person amidst the multitude of demands and pressures of ministry. We face not only unrealistic expectations of others and ourselves, but our own inadequacy as well. In this study of 2 Corinthians and the Old Testament prophets, we are brought back to the God who makes us adequate as His servants in the new covenant.

How is it possible in our day to be sustained in ministry here at home or on the mission field amidst the great challenges we face from within and without? Author Bill Mills has given great hope to all of us who desire to be faithful by directing us to the living Word of our God, which is able to revive our very souls. There we encounter none other than our sovereign God and loving Father. We can join our hearts with the psalmist and say of our Lord, "He is my refuge and my fortress, my God, in whom I trust" (Psalm 91:2, NIV). It is in the nourishing Word of God that our hope in the Lord can be renewed as we see our sovereign and glorious God. In these, we are reminded that our sufficiency lies not in ourselves but rather in the fullness of the Lord Jesus Christ.

We are "God's workmanship, created in Christ Jesus to do good works, which God prepared in advance for us to do" (Ephesians 2:10, NIV). The same God who called us to Himself not only has prepared us for ministry but also has preordained the ministry given to each of us in the unique and special sphere in which we serve. God has given us the inestimable privilege of being co-ministers with Him, undershepherds of the Great Shepherd as we faithfully seek to fulfill His will for our lives.

My hope and prayer are that our Lord may use this book to bring great encouragement to your heart and deep joy to your soul as you serve none other than God Himself and the Church of our Lord Jesus Christ.

Rev. Hutz H. Hertzberg, D.Min.
Administrative Pastor, Moody Church
Chicago, Illinois

The earth will be filled with the knowledge of the glory of the LORD as the waters cover the sea.

Habakkuk 2:14

Introduction:
An Eternal Stewardship

Adequate! God has made us competent for all He has set before us! This is good news for all of us who have struggled with a deep sense of inadequacy as we are confronted with ministry opportunities. The call is so big—walking with God as He is filling the earth with His glory—and we are so small. Whether God has called us to give actions to our faith, to preach, to counsel, or to encourage, we continually face our great inadequacies. We are not eloquent enough. We are not spiritual enough. We do not know the Bible well enough. We do not have enough faith.

It is encouraging to know that we are not alone in this battle. As the apostle Paul more fully understood the ministry God had set before him, he cried,

Who is sufficient for these things? (2 Corinthians 2:16b)

None of us is equal to what God has set before us to do. Not one of us is adequate in ourselves. We know all too well the truth of Jesus' statement to His disciples:

Adequate!

Apart from me you can do nothing. (John 15:5b)

The glorious news of the gospel is that we are not only saved from sin and justified by a righteous God, but we are also filled with His very life in His Son. Christ now becomes our resource for life and godliness, for serving God and one another. His life within us encourages us to walk in all that our Father sets before us. Paul summarizes this great truth as he talks of his steward-ship before the church:

> To them God chose to make known how great among the Gentiles are the riches of the glory of this mystery, which is Christ in you, the hope of glory. (Colossians 1:27)

Now we are able, in Christ, to walk in great power and to fully serve God in all that He gives us to do. Our competence comes from Him, not from ourselves. Paul touched on this truth in his Philippian letter as well:

> I can do all things through him who strengthens me. (Philippians 4:13)

In His Son, God has entrusted to us a great work, a ministry completely dependent on the resource of His life within us. When Jesus Christ returned to His Father, He committed to His disciples the ministry He had begun. God had sent Him as the means of reconciling the world to Himself. Now, with that work accomplished in the release of His life at the cross, the continuing process of ministering God's life in this world would be fulfilled through those whom He had chosen for that work. You and I are part of that life-giving chain of God's chosen ones down through history. What God has done within us, He is now fulfilling through us in the midst of this world.

CHRIST IS GOD'S MEANS OF MINISTRY

Ministry is God giving His life to men and women, even to those who have been cut off from Him by the rebellion of their sin. The means by which God gives Himself to us is His own Son. God has sent His Son into the world as the fullness of all that He is, the vessel of His life to us. Paul reveals this great truth about who Christ is as he prays for the Colossian Christians

> that their hearts may be encouraged, being knit together in love, to reach all the riches of full assurance of understanding and the knowledge of God's mystery, which is Christ, in whom are hidden all the treasures of wisdom and knowledge....See to it that no one takes you captive by philosophy and empty deceit, according to human tradition, according to the elemental spirits of the world, and not according to Christ. For in him the whole fullness of deity dwells bodily, and you have been filled in him, who is the head of all rule and authority. (Colossians 2:2-3, 8-10)

The Lord had spoken through the prophet Isaiah about how He would change the lives of His people by His sovereign power and His abundant mercy, giving hope to those who too long had lived in darkness and despair.

> The Spirit of the Lord GOD is upon me, because the LORD has anointed me to bring good news to the poor; he has sent me to bind up the brokenhearted, to proclaim liberty to the captives, and the opening of the prison to those who are bound; to proclaim the year of the LORD's favor, and the day of vengeance of our God; to comfort all who mourn; to grant to those who mourn in Zion—to give them a beautiful headdress instead of ashes the oil of gladness instead of mourning, the garment of praise instead of a faint spirit; that they may be called oaks of righteousness, the planting of the LORD, that he may be glorified. (Isaiah 61:1-3)

Adequate!

God desires to bring the good news of His healing love to those who hurt deeply but are willing to listen to His voice, to place His strong arms around those whose hearts have been crushed by the pressures and the pain of this world, and to hold them close to Himself. God enables those who have been chained to failure and sin to now walk in freedom and light. For those whose hearts have been broken by the awareness of their sin against a holy God, the compassionate love of the Savior brings peace, and His power is seen in their own person in a new creation. Instead of death and brokenness, God gives them life and joy; in the place of despair and fear before the living God, they are filled with the ability to praise Him. Those who receive the ministry of life from the Creator become strong, deeply rooted oaks who are able by God's power to demonstrate to the world what is right and holy.

God takes those who are weak, whose lives are filled with pain, who have no hope left in this system, and He transforms them into "oaks of righteousness." What a picture of strength, stability, fruitfulness and holiness! It is the planting of the Lord for the display of His splendor. This work begins in the heart of God and flows through us in a way that returns to Him, and He is glorified. I hope that this is something we return to again and again in our time of study together: Only what comes from God can result in His glory.

Some seven hundred years after the prophet Isaiah wrote those words under the inspiration of the Holy Spirit, Jesus Christ, the Father's means of fulfilling this prophecy, stood in the synagogue in Nazareth and read the same verses from the scroll of Isaiah; then,

> he rolled up the scroll and gave it back to the attendant and sat down. And the eyes of all in the synagogue were fixed on him. And he began to say to them, "Today this Scripture has been ful-filled in your hearing." (Luke 4:20-21)

The only thing Jesus has added to what Isaiah recorded is the opening of blind eyes to see. Jesus, the Light of the world, has come, and now our blind eyes can see as He touches us with His healing power. The Light has entered the realm of darkness! God has turned on His Light in a world that cannot see anything clearly and has sent the One who will enable men to see themselves, their Creator, and the people and things around them through His eyes. Today God is still fulfilling this ministry of His Son through us.

THE CROSS IS THE WAY

Jesus Christ is the fullness of the Life of God that we so desperately need. The cross is the way God makes His life available to us. Christ lived a life of complete obedience to His Father, demonstrating for His disciples a life of holiness, obedience, and righteousness. However, we were in need of more than an example if we, too, were to be able to live godly lives; we needed the very power of God's life within us. Jesus Christ, the vessel through whom God poured out His life, was willing to be broken in order for us to share in the life of God.

> To this you have been called, because Christ also suffered for you, leaving you an example, so that you might follow in his steps. He committed no sin, neither was deceit found in his mouth. When he was reviled, he did not revile in return; when he suffered, he did not threaten, but continued entrusting himself to him who judges justly. He himself bore our sins in his body on the tree, that we might die to sin and live to righteousness. By his wounds you have been healed. For you were straying like sheep, but have now returned to the Shepherd and Overseer of your souls. (1 Peter 2:21-25)

There was no way apart from the cross of Christ that God's life could be poured out to men and women. The fact that the Son of

17

Adequate!

God was willing to give His life for the enemies of God is some-thing we will never be able to comprehend. From Genesis three through the entirety of His Word, God has taught that after the entrance of sin in human history, life must be given in order for life to be sustained. That is one purpose of animal sacrifice; the vivid picture of eating the flesh of animals to sustain our own life in this world. Because of sin, our lives are sustained only at the expense of other life. All of this points to the ultimate demonstra-tion of how God gives His life to us. His life must be poured out if men are to live. As God calls us to be vessels through which He will continue to minister His life to people, He calls us to pour out our lives as well.

> Truly, truly, I say to you, unless a grain of wheat falls into the earth and dies, it remains alone; but if it dies, it bears much fruit. Whoever loves his life loses it, and whoever hates his life in this world will keep it for eternal life. If anyone serves me, he must follow me; and where I am, there will my servant be also. If anyone serves me, the Father will honor him. (John 12:24-26)

There is no other path to ministry than the way of the cross. That was God's answer to His own Son in the Garden of Geth-semane, and that is His answer to us as we come to Him. Paul wrote to the Corinthians about the ministry of God's life through His Son and about our being vessels of Jesus' life and death.

> We have this treasure in jars of clay, to show that the surpassing power belongs to God and not to us. We are afflicted in every way, but not crushed; perplexed, but not driven to despair; perse-cuted, but not forsaken; struck down, but not destroyed; always carrying in the body the death of Jesus, so that the life of Jesus may also be manifested in our bodies. For we who live are always being given over to death for Jesus' sake, so that the life of Jesus also may be manifested in our mortal flesh. (2 Corinthians 4:7-11)

OUR MINISTRY OF CHRIST'S LIFE TO OTHERS

Because of the cross, we are part of the process throughout history in which God is giving His life to men and women. The apostle Paul, fully aware of the cost to his own life of following Christ and yet filled with a sense of joy and purpose in being an eternal partner with the living God, wrote to the Christians at Colossae about what God is accomplishing in history:

> I rejoice in my sufferings for your sake, and in my flesh I am filling up what is lacking in Christ's afflictions for the sake of his body, that is, the church, of which I became a minister according to the stewardship from God that was given to me for you, to make the word of God fully known, the mystery hidden for ages and generations but now revealed to his saints. To them God chose to make known how great among the Gentiles are the riches of the glory of this mystery, which is Christ in you, the hope of glory. (Colossians 1:24-27)

Paul saw himself as a steward of the mysteries of God. Now in these last days, God is revealing to us how He gives Himself to us and enables us to live lives of godliness. The message entrusted to Paul and to us is not limited to moral demonstration or to theological instruction; the heart of that message and that life itself is the indwelling of His own Son! Our message is "Christ in you the hope of glory" because we believe in the Holy Spirit. We are no longer limited by who we are, by what we are able to do, or by our personalities or education. What we become is based on who Christ is and on what God is able to do in us through Him.

Paul understood ministry in terms of God's giving His life to His people through His Son, and he knew that God had called him as a vessel through whom to continue that process. It was Paul's desire to fulfill that ministry to every man and woman, in every way, to bring them to maturity in Christ. God has called you and me to share in the eternal stewardship of the ministry of His life in this world. By His grace and by the power of the living God within us, let us join with Paul and all who have walked as God's servants before us, as open vessels, committed in every way to the work God desires to accomplish through us. It is a work that will end not only in the salvation of those whom God is seeking but also in the worship of the redeemed throughout eternity.

> Him we proclaim, warning everyone and teaching everyone with all wisdom, that we may present everyone mature in Christ. For this I toil, struggling with all his energy that he powerfully works within me. (Colossians 1:28-29)

When the apostle Paul wrote to the church at Corinth, he helped us to understand how God pours His life through us into this world. He also enabled us to see who we are in relationship with God along the way. Can anything else fill us with such a sense of value as Paul's words given here by the Holy Spirit? What hope is ours in ministry when we see ourselves through the eyes of God!

> Working together with him, then, we appeal to you not to receive the grace of God in vain. (2 Corinthians 6:1)

We who were dead in our sins, slaves of sin and even enemies of God, He has redeemed through the blood of His own Son. But He has not only forgiven us through the cross; God has also made us His children, called us His friends, and named us as His co-workers. How surprising of our great God to humble Himself in order to elevate us in this way!

As we ponder God's "co-workers" through the ages, we not only see God's humility but also gain a glimpse of His sovereignty as He builds His Kingdom that will never pass away. When we consider Abraham, Moses and David, or when we look at the apostles Peter and Paul and remember the saints through history, we are reminded that our God is able to fulfill all of His will, even with weak people who come to Him with all their hearts.

We follow in their train. Our God is the same yesterday, today, and forever; He is still sufficient when we are small. The Holy Spirit lives within us and empowers us, so we can still be confident when we are weak. Because the love of Christ compels us, because of the joy we find in Him, and so that the Bride of Christ might reflect the beauty of her Lord for all eternity, let us serve our God with all the strength He supplies until His glory fills the earth!

Moses said, "Please show me your glory." And he said, "I will make all my goodness pass before you and will proclaim before you my name 'The LORD.' And I will be gracious to whom I will be gracious, and will show mercy on whom I will show mercy."

Exodus 33:18-19

1
Vision and Ministry

Suppose one of the young people in our youth group, one with a whole heart for the Lord, came to us and said, "I want God to use me; I want to serve the Lord and bear fruit that will last forever; how should I prepare for that kind of ministry?" What would we tell that young person?

Now, suppose we were able to take that young man or woman right into the presence of the Lord to be introduced and say, "Father, this is such a special young person with a great desire to be used for Your glory; how should he or she spend the next years preparing for a ministry that would glorify your name throughout all eternity?" How would God respond?

Would God say, "The first thing you need to do is get the best education you possibly can. Your education will lay the foundation for your career, and the better you are educated, the more effectively I will be able to use you."? Or would God say, "Study theology. The more effectively you can handle the ancient writings and the Scriptures and apply them to the questions people are asking, the more effectively I will use you in the building of my church"? Or would God say, "Study psychology. You are living in a painful and competitive world in which people around you have more pain in their lives than they can handle. The more you can touch people in the places they are hurting, the more effectively I will be able to use you"? Or maybe God would say, "Study technology. I have caused you to live in a time in which there are tools available for ministry and the proclamation of the gospel that people a few years ago hardly even dreamed would be available. And the more effectively you can handle those tools, the more effectively I will be able to use you."

God would not say any of that, would He? What God would say is, "Your ministry and your life will become fruitful and effective to the degree that you learn to see me." I believe that is what God would say because that is what He said to Moses, to Jeremiah, to Ezekiel, and to the apostle Paul. Have you noticed as you have studied the Scriptures how often God begins ministry with vision? That vision is not focused on what He will do through us as much as it is a vision of Himself. When we talk about vision, our eyes are often filled with all that we would do; when God talks about vision, He is talking about our eyes being filled with who He is. That is the vision with which God begins ministry.

A VISION OF GOD'S HOLINESS

When God called the prophet Isaiah, He began that young man's ministry with a vision of His holiness. Isaiah recorded that call in chapter 6 of the book that bears his name:

> In the year that King Uzziah died I saw the Lord sitting upon a throne, high and lifted up; and the train of his robe filled the temple. (Isaiah 6:1)

Isaiah then began to describe the scene around the throne of God. The angels there proclaim God's holiness to Him and to one another: "Holy, holy, holy is the LORD" is their cry!

> Above him stood the seraphim. Each had six wings: with two he covered his face, and with two he covered his feet, and with two he flew. And one called to another and said: "Holy, holy, holy is the LORD of hosts; the whole earth is full of his glory!" (Isaiah 6:2-3)

If we are leading a group Bible study on the attributes of God and begin by saying "Let's list the attributes of God," we probably would begin with love, because that is what we often assume is the central attribute of God. In most groups we would go on to talk about God's mercy, His compassion, His justice, His power, and His grace. It probably would be a while before we listed holiness. That is not the way it is with the angels that surround God's throne! Of all the characteristics of God, it is his purity, His complete separation from everything evil, the fact that He is "other" than what we are in every way—these are what captivate the angels that surround His throne. That is what fills their eyes and becomes their vision and their message. They proclaim, "Holy, holy, holy is the LORD."

No other attribute of God in all His Word receives the three-fold affirmation and proclamation that His holiness receives. Neither His love nor His power, His majesty nor His justice, receives that level of worship. It is His holiness that the angels proclaim! When we come to the book of Revelation and see the scene around the throne of God, the message that is proclaimed once more is "Holy, holy, holy is the Lord God Almighty" (Revelation 4:8).

How would your life and your ministry be different if your eyes and your heart were filled with a vision of the holiness of

Adequate!

God? How would that affect the way you see Him, yourself, your sin, and the sins of others? A vision of God in His holiness transforms our view of God, the way in which we see ourselves, and our attitude toward sin. I have struggled with sin in my life, as perhaps you have. I have tried everything I have ever heard of and every formula I ever came across to defeat it. Nothing ever moved me from sin except a vision of the holiness of God. As He did with Isaiah, God will call us and prepare us for ministry with a vision of His holiness.

A Vision of God's Glory

God's call of Ezekiel to the ministry of a prophet also began with vision:

> In the thirtieth year, in the fourth month, on the fifth day of the month, as I was among the exiles by the Chebar canal, the heavens were opened, and I saw visions of God. (Ezekiel 1:1)

Although Ezekiel goes on to talk about his vision of the beings and the wheels, look with me as his vision comes to a crescendo in the display of God's glory.

> Above the expanse over their heads there was the likeness of a throne, in appearance like sapphire; and seated above the likeness of a throne was a likeness with a human appearance. And upward from what had the appearance of his waist I saw as it were gleaming metal, like the appearance of fire enclosed all around. And downward from what had the appearance of his waist I saw as it were the appearance of fire, and there was brightness around him. Like the appearance of the bow that is in the cloud on the day of rain, so was the appearance of the brightness all around. Such was the appearance of the likeness of the glory of the LORD. And when I saw it, I fell on my face, and I heard the voice of one speaking. (Ezekiel 1:26-28)

God began the ministry of the prophet Ezekiel by giving him a vision of His glory. How would your life and your ministry be different if always filling your eyes and your heart was a vision of God's radiant beauty and the weight of His presence? How would that affect the way you look at the glory of who you are and what you are able to produce? How would that affect the way you see the glory of this world?

You might remember how Satan came to the Lord Jesus and tempted Him with the glories of all the kingdoms of this world. "If you, then, will worship me, it will all be yours," Satan tells the Lord Jesus (Luke 4:7). Satan was seeking to cause Jesus to circumvent God's way to His glory by distracting Him with the glory of this world. God's way to glory was Jesus' laying down His life, the way of the cross. Satan was hoping Jesus would be vulnerable to a plan to "shortcut the process," but Jesus' eyes were filled with a vision of God's glory, and He pressed on to its fulfillment even through the cross.

This world manifests great and glorious things. There is glory in our technological accomplishments, our space explorations, our charitable efforts, our sports triumphs, and our medical achievements. How will God move us to walk with Him in the fulfillment of His will without a vision of His glory that surpasses the glories of this world? What is the center of His purposes? The prophet Habakkuk revealed that to us:

> The earth will be filled with the knowledge of the glory of the LORD as the waters cover the sea. (Habakkuk 2:14)

God's ultimate purpose is that the radiance of His Person would fill all His realms and His works. He will move us to walk with Him in that ministry as He fills us with the vision of His glory. As he desired in tempting Jesus, Satan desires to steal away our ability to walk with God in the fulfillment of His pur-

Adequate!

poses by giving us a vision of the glory of our accomplishments and of what the world will produce. But as God did for Ezekiel, He will captivate us with a vision of His glory, and then we will walk with Him in the fulfillment of His great eternal works.

A Vision of God's All-sufficient Power

I would like you to think with me for a moment of Moses, God's chosen deliverer, when His people were enslaved in Egypt. You might remember that God had prepared Moses over a period of many years for the task He would set before him. Moses was protected by God in his birth, raised in wealth and security in Pharaoh's family, and given the best education available in the world. However, in the midst of all this, Moses was a failure in this world. Guilty of murder, he ran for his life to the land of Midian where he became a shepherd. During those years the Israelites were suffering as slaves in Egypt, and the Lord heard their cry for a redeemer:

> During those many days the king of Egypt died, and the people of Israel groaned because of their slavery and cried out for help. Their cry for rescue from slavery came up to God. And God heard their groaning, and God remembered his covenant with Abraham, with Isaac, and with Jacob. (Exodus 2:23-24)

One day, as Moses was shepherding the flock that God had provided for him,

> The angel of the LORD appeared to him in a flame of fire out of the midst of a bush. He looked, and behold, the bush was burning, yet it was not consumed. (Exodus 3:2)

Moses' response was to turn aside, but the Lord called to him from the bush:

"Moses, Moses!" And he said, "Here I am." Then he said, "Do not come near; take your sandals off your feet, for the place on which you are standing is holy ground." And he said, "I am the God of your father, the God of Abraham, the God of Isaac, and the God of Jacob." And Moses hid his face, for he was afraid to look at God. (Exodus 3:4b-6)

God revealed to Moses that He was aware of His people's pain and suffering and that Moses would be the man He would use to deliver them:

Now, behold, the cry of the people of Israel has come to me, and I have also seen the oppression with which the Egyptians oppress them. Come, I will send you to Pharaoh that you may bring my people, the children of Israel, out of Egypt. (Exodus 3:9-10)

Moses responded to God's call in a typically human way, saying to God, "But who am I?" He was immediately confronted with his own inadequacy to fulfill what God had called him to do. Then Moses asked a far more significant question of God: "Who are You?" Who God is becomes the means by which we come to know ourselves, and it becomes the basis for our ministry, as it did for Moses.

God said to Moses, "I AM WHO I AM." And he said, "Say this to the people of Israel, 'I AM has sent me to you.'" God also said to Moses, "Say this to the people of Israel, 'The LORD, the God of your fathers, the God of Abraham, the God of Isaac, and the God of Jacob, has sent me to you.' This is my name forever, and thus I am to be remembered throughout all generations." (Exodus 3:14-15)

God revealed Himself to Moses as the ever-present, ever-living, all-sufficient God of Abraham, Isaac, and Jacob. The God of the fathers of Israel is the same God who hears the cries of His people and is able to deliver them. God is saying to Moses, "I am the source of everything you need in ministry. I am your strength; I am your adequacy; I am the love you need for My people; I am your confidence, your patience and your power."

Then Moses began to argue with God about all that might go wrong in this overwhelming ministry, expressing his own fears and lack of confidence. "What if the people will not believe me? I am not eloquent enough to do that ministry."

> Then the LORD said to him, "Who has made man's mouth? Who makes him mute, or deaf, or seeing, or blind? Is it not I, the LORD? Now therefore go, and I will be with your mouth and teach you what you shall speak." But he said, "Oh, my Lord, please send someone else." (Exodus 4:11-13)

Moses had come to the conclusion that he was not able to do the work God had set before him because of his own weakness and inadequacy. God wanted to confirm in Moses' understanding the fact that effective ministry depends not on who we are and what we are able to do but on who God is and what He is able to do. This is why God began Moses' ministry with a vision of Himself. Just as God filled a bush with His power and fire, He would fill Moses. He will do the same for you and me. The scope and depth of our ministry will flow out of how we see Him; the fuller our view of God, the fuller our ministry will be.

How would your life and your ministry be changed if your eyes and your heart were filled with the vision of God's sufficiency, the greatness of His power? How would that affect the way you respond to ministry opportunities? How often, when we have the opportunity to share our faith with someone, to teach a Bible class, to take a position of leadership, or to counsel or serve someone, are we overwhelmed with our weaknesses! Satan uses our sense of inadequacy to cause us to retreat from ministry opportunities. He steals our boldness away. Satan wants us to see ourselves through his eyes, in light of all we are not! But God calls us to see all our sufficiency in Him. We will never have boldness and freedom in ministry without a vision of God's all-sufficient power. Only with that vision will we have confidence that whatever God sets before us He will fulfill for the glory of His name.

A VISION OF CHRIST'S LORDSHIP

When I think of Moses, I think of the apostle Paul. Paul is the contrast to Moses in so many ways. Moses was consumed with a sense of inadequacy; Paul was a supremely confident man. Even before he was a Christian, he thought he knew what God was doing. He believed that God had raised him up to destroy this new sect of believers in Jesus. When he was on the road to Damascus for that very purpose, God knocked him to the ground as the bright light of Christ shone upon him. God invaded Paul's life and laid hold of his will and his heart.

Do you remember what Paul's first words were as he lay in that blinding light? "Who are you, Lord?" That vision of the lordship of Jesus never left Paul's heart. It was sealed in the center of his soul. Again and again we read in Paul's letters, "Paul, a bondservant of the Lord; Paul, a bondservant of Jesus." God will make the same of you and me.

How would your life and your ministry be different if a vision of the lordship of Jesus filled your eyes and your heart? How would that affect the choices you make from day to day? How would it affect the way in which you look at the options for your life and the freedom you have to go in a certain direction or become involved in various pursuits? As with the apostle Paul, all our choices, our goals, and our dreams are wiped away in a vision of Jesus as Lord. For Paul, this meant living as a "bondser-

31

vant" all his days, the possession of the One who had purchased him with His own blood. So it will be for you and me.

A Vision of God's Sovereignty

As you know, the book of Job begins with the angels of God presenting themselves before the Lord, and Satan is walking among them. It is not Satan who brings up the subject of Job; it is God. He says to the enemy, "Have you considered my servant, Job?"

> Satan answered the LORD and said, "Does Job fear God for no reason? Have you not put a hedge around him and his house and all that he has, on every side? You have blessed the work of his hands, and his possessions have increased in the land. But stretch out your hand and touch all that he has, and he will curse you to your face." (Job 1:9-11)

So God gave Satan permission to interfere in Job's life. Of course, Satan never could have touched Job without God's permission. A great battle began to take place. Job lost his health, his wealth, his family, and his bearings. Three friends came to counsel him and brought him man's perspective on his circumstances and his experiences. Then God brought to Job another young man, Elihu, with His own perspective. Toward the end of the book, however, we find some of the most unique verses in all the Word of God. In those verses, God personally came to Job and began to draw word pictures in his mind and heart so that he could see God in His exalted glory and splendor and in His sovereign control over His creation:

> The LORD answered Job out of the whirlwind and said: "Who is this that darkens counsel by words without knowledge? Dress for action like a man; I will question you, and you make it known to me." (Job 38:1-3)

In his pain and loss, Job had begun to see himself out of proportion in his relationship with God. He has been reacting to God, reaching for answers, expecting explanations. Now God says, "I will ask the questions, Job. *You* provide the answers!"

> Where were you when I laid the foundation of the earth? Tell me, if you have understanding. Who determined its measurements—surely you know! Or who stretched the line upon it? On what were its bases sunk, or who laid its cornerstone, when the morning stars sang together and all the sons of God shouted for joy? Or who shut in the sea with doors when it burst out from the womb...? (Job 38:4-8)

God is opening Job's eyes so that he can see His transcendence above all His creation, and His sovereignty over all His works.

> Have you commanded the morning since your days began, and caused the dawn to know its place...? (Job 38:12)

Job, when was the last time you commanded the morning? What would you say if God asked you that question? You would probably say, "I haven't done that lately, Lord!"

> Can you lead forth the Mazzaroth in their season, or can you guide the Bear with its children? Do you know the ordinances of the heavens? Can you establish their rule on the earth? (Job 38:32-33)

We have four chapters of that kind of challenge, in which God comes to Job in a very personal, intimate, even overwhelming way and draws these word pictures so that Job can see His greatness and His sovereignty over all.

Job responds in the beginning of chapter 42:

> Job answered the LORD and said: "I know that you can do all things, and that no purpose of yours can be thwarted." (Job 42:1-2)

Adequate!

Can you imagine a purer confession coming from the heart of any person than what Job has said? "God, I know that you can do anything you choose to do, and no one can keep you from fulfilling your purposes."

> "'Who is this that hides counsel without knowledge?' Therefore I have uttered what I did not understand, things too wonderful for me, which I did not know. 'Hear, and I will speak; I will question you, and you make it known to me.' I had heard of you by the hearing of the ear, but now my eye sees you; therefore I despise myself, and repent in dust and ashes." (Job 42:3-6)

Job's life and heart were transformed in the midst of his pain and his loss as God opened to him a vision of His sovereign control over all His creation and over all Job's life. God will transform our hearts, our lives, and our ministries in a vision of His sovereignty. When we see the greatness of God, God will do great things through us and enable us to rest in Him in the process.

Job said, "I had heard of you…but now my eye sees you" (Job 42:5). His life was transformed as he saw God. In our educational systems, most of our learning comes by way of hearing. But it is what we see that moves us in life. Just like Job, our lives will be transformed as our vision of God grows.

How Do We See God?

Like the prophets, we must see God. And as He did with these men of old, God will begin our walk with Him and our ministries with a vision of Himself. How does He do that? How is it that we receive a vision of God? God reveals Himself to us through His written Word, the Scriptures, and through the living Word, Jesus, through the ministry of the Holy Spirit.

Solomon said to his son:

My son, if you receive my words and treasure up my commandments with you, making your ear attentive to wisdom and inclining your heart to understanding; yes, if you call out for insight and raise your voice for understanding, if you seek it like silver and search for it as for hidden treasures, then you will understand the fear of the LORD and find the knowledge of God. (Proverbs 2:1-5)

The written Word points us to the knowledge of God. The fullness of that revelation is in Christ, the Messiah.

In the beginning was the Word, and the Word was with God, and the Word was God....And the Word became flesh and dwelt among us, and we have seen his glory, glory as of the only Son from the Father, full of grace and truth. (John 1:1,14)

The writer to the Hebrews teaches us that Jesus reveals the Father:

He is the radiance of the glory of God and the exact imprint of his nature, and he upholds the universe by the word of his power. After making purification for sins, he sat down at the right hand of the Majesty on high, having become as much superior to angels as the name he has inherited is more excellent than theirs. (Hebrews 1:3-4)

In Jesus we see God the Father. Jesus is the exact representation of His being! Paul described Jesus to the church at Colossae in this way:

In him the whole fullness of deity dwells bodily. (Colossians 2:9)

All that God is, living in a body—that is who Jesus is. Jesus made this very clear to us in response to His disciple Philip's question:

Philip said to [Jesus], "Lord, show us the Father, and it is enough for us." Jesus said to him, "Have I been with you so long, and you

35

still do not know me, Philip? Whoever has seen me has seen the Father. How can you say, 'Show us the Father'?" (John 14:8-9)

Jesus is the means by which we come to know God. In fact, Jesus prayed in John 17:

> This is eternal life, that they know you the only true God, and Jesus Christ whom you have sent. (John 17:3)

Jesus is the only way to see and know God; apart from Him there is no true knowledge of God beyond the general revelation of creation. The ministry of the Holy Spirit is to open our eyes and our hearts to a growing understanding of who Jesus is through the Scriptures, so that we can see Him and the Father He reveals more fully and be transformed in His presence.

> When the Spirit of truth comes, he will guide you into all the truth, for he will not speak on his own authority, but whatever he hears he will speak, and he will declare to you the things that are to come. He will glorify me, for he will take what is mine and declare it to you. All that the Father has is mine; therefore I said that he will take what is mine and declare it to you. (John 16:13-15)

TWO TREES

I would like you to go back with me to the early chapters of Genesis. You will remember how God created Adam and Eve and placed them in the beautiful Garden of Eden, an environment in which they could enjoy everything God had made and even walk with Him as His co-workers in His creation. There were two trees in the middle of that garden. One was the Tree of Life, and the other was the tree of the knowledge of good and evil. God called Adam and Eve to come continually to the Tree of Life, and there they would be able to draw all their life from Him. God would be the source for their lives. Everything they needed intellectually, emotionally, physically, and spiritually would be found in Him. However, God told them to not eat from the tree of the knowledge of good and evil.

Now from the very fact that God called them to eat from the Tree of Life and forbade them to eat from the tree of the knowledge of good and evil, we know that God is saying to them, "It is much better to know Me than to know everything else there is to know." In the environment of Satan's temptation, they made the wrong choice. They chose to eat from the tree of the knowledge of good and evil. Satan had said, "You can become like God (whom you admire; no need to get rid of God, just get along with Him as equals)." By following him, they could find in themselves all they needed—or so he wanted them to believe.

Throughout history, the choices of Adam and Eve have been reflected in the choices of every generation. We are still eating from the wrong tree. We are living in the midst of the greatest knowledge explosion this world has ever known. We cannot even begin to assimilate the knowledge we are gaining from day to day! What is happening in the field of space exploration reveals this truth. We can send spaceships to the outer reaches of our solar system, take pictures of what is in the rings of Saturn and send them back in moments. In the field of medicine we see new discoveries day after day. Mushrooming capability in the field of computers is a vivid reminder of our knowledge explosion. If you buy a computer, start immediately saving for your next one because in a very brief time it will be obsolete! Our technologies are becoming more glorious with every passing day.

Has all this knowledge and information been able to penetrate the dark depravity of our hearts? We seem incapable in our human efforts to place limits on the hatred, evil, and pain we bring on one another in this world. Racism, economic injustice, and tribal warfare continue to devastate entire nations and cultures. We seem to be driven by greed and the pursuits of power and pleasure rather than by a desire for justice and mercy.

God is still saying to us, "You might not understand all the implications of this, but you must believe Me: It is better to know Me than it is to possess the sum total of all the knowledge and information this world can give to you. It is better to know Me than to know everything else there is to know."

LIFT UP YOUR EYES

Our view of God is the basis from which all our lives flow. How we see God is the axis on which all our lives turn. Every thought and feeling we have; every word we speak; every choice we make; all our values, motives, priorities, and relationships flow directly from our view of God. All our lives and all our ministries will be the result of how we see Him.

In Isaiah 40, we see God's desire to comfort His hurting, captive people:

Comfort, comfort my people, says your God. (Isaiah 40:1)

How will God comfort His people? He begins to open their eyes so they can see Him in His exalted power and glory:

To whom then will you liken God, or what likeness compare with him? An idol! A craftsman casts it, and a goldsmith overlays it with gold and casts for it silver chains. He who is too impoverished for an offering chooses wood that will not rot; he seeks out a skillful craftsman to set up an idol that will not move. (Isaiah 40:18-20)

God confronts His people with an age-old question: "Will you reduce the Lord of glory to an image made with hands? Will you worship what you have made rather than the God who has made the world and revealed Himself in His Word and in His creation?"

Do you not know? Do you not hear? Has it not been told you from the beginning? Have you not understood from the foundations of the earth? It is he who sits above the circle of the earth, and its inhabitants are like grasshoppers; who stretches out the heavens like a curtain, and spreads them like a tent to dwell in; (Isaiah 40:21-22)

Again God confronts His people with a question that must grip their hearts: "To what other god will you compare me? Is there any equal to me in earth or heaven? Lift up your eyes and see me!"

To whom then will you compare me, that I should be like him? says the Holy One. Lift up your eyes on high and see: who created these? He who brings out their host by number, calling them all by name, by the greatness of his might, and because he is strong in power not one is missing. Why do you say, O Jacob, and speak, O Israel, "My way is hidden from the LORD, and my right is disregarded by my God"? (Isaiah 40:25-27)

Sometimes in our hopelessness, pain, and loss, we find ourselves in this same place. We feel that God is not aware of what is going on in our lives; we are cut off from Him. But God encourages us that He, the living God, the Creator of the ends of the earth, is intimately involved in our life experiences.

Have you not known? Have you not heard? The LORD is the everlasting God, the Creator of the ends of the earth. He does not faint or grow weary; his understanding is unsearchable. He gives power to the faint, and to him who has no might he increases strength. Even youths shall faint and be weary, and young men shall fall exhausted; but they who wait for the LORD shall renew their strength; they shall mount up with wings like eagles; they shall run and not be weary; they shall walk and not faint. (Isaiah 40:28-31)

How does God comfort His hurting people? He comforts them by giving them an expanded vision of who He is. As they see God

Adequate!

in the fullness of His power and His glory, His strength becomes their own. As God lifts their eyes to see Him, He pours His life and His power into them. As His people hope in Him, they soar on wings like eagles. They run without becoming weary and walk without fainting. As they experience an exalted view of God, He transforms the hearts of His people. So it is with you and me. All our lives and all our ministries will flow out of how we see God.

A Vision of Ourselves

Our view of ourselves overflows from our vision of God. When we see God, we see ourselves. The psalmist wrote,

> With you is the fountain of life; in your light do we see light. (Psalm 36:9)

Our view of ourselves is the result of our vision of God. We can never know ourselves without knowing God first. In the light of who God is, our knowledge of ourselves grows. We saw that in the prophet Isaiah. His response in that vision of the holiness of God is to see himself through God's eyes:

> "Woe is me! For I am lost; for I am a man of unclean lips, and I dwell in the midst of a people of unclean lips; for my eyes have seen the King, the LORD of hosts!" (Isaiah 6:5)

When Isaiah saw God in His holiness and His glory, he saw his own sins and the sins of his people. Only when we see God, do we see ourselves clearly. The Scriptures give us a very full and realistic picture of who we are. Jesus said to His disciples,

> I am the vine; you are the branches. Whoever abides in me and I in him, he it is that bears much fruit, for apart from me you can do nothing. (John 15:5)

The apostle Paul wrote to the church at Philippi:

I can do all things through him who strengthens me. (Philippians 4:13)

That is a realistic understanding of who we are—completely incapable apart from God, completely sufficient when Christ is within us!

One of the great battles of our lives is learning to see ourselves through the eyes of God. Our enemy desires that we see ourselves in light of our past, our feelings, and our failures. It is a great turning point when we see ourselves through the eyes of our Father, when we take hold of who He says we are and begin walking in that light with great freedom and boldness. Often, when God reveals to us who we are in His eyes, we tend to shrink back and say to ourselves, "That cannot be true. That is not what I am." Paul wrote to the church at Colossae, and to you and me, "You are holy; you are loved" (see Colossians 3:12). He wrote to the church at Rome, "You are free from sin" (see Romans 6:7). God tells us that He has given us all we need for life and godliness (see 2 Peter 1:4). Often when we read these great truths, we say, "God, this cannot be true; this is not who I am."

There are times when we refuse to believe what God says about us, and instead we believe the lies of the enemy or our own feelings. What a great victory it is, then, when we believe we are who God says we are, affirm it, and walk in confidence.

One of our favorite Bible characters is Gideon, the champion that God raised up to set the people free when they were oppressed under the Midianites. Do you remember how God found Gideon? As the angel of the Lord came to Gideon, he was hiding in the winepress, threshing grain:

The angel of the LORD appeared to him and said to him, "The LORD is with you, O mighty man of valor." (Judges 6:12)

We tend to laugh when we read this, because if Gideon were really a mighty warrior, he would be out doing battle with the enemy instead of hiding in the winepress! At some point in this story, however, we must ask this, "Who is right about Gideon? Is God right about Gideon, or is Gideon right about Gideon?" Before the story is over, we know the answer to that question. God is right about Gideon. Gideon *is* a mighty warrior. That is who God is calling him to be and making him to be, and Gideon must walk in that truth, placing his confidence in God.

We must also walk in this truth, because God is right about who we are. First we see God in His holiness, His glory, and His power, and then we see ourselves through His eyes. God transforms our view of ourselves in a vision of who He is.

A Vision of Others

Our lives and our ministries flow from our ever-growing vision of God. The more fully we see Him, the more clearly we will see ourselves. Then God will give us the grace to see other people through His eyes:

> The love of Christ controls us, because we have concluded this: that one has died for all, therefore all have died. (2 Corinthians 5:14)

How does God motivate us in ministry? Does He manipulate us with guilt, fear, or pressure? No, He compels us with His love! God's love for us and our response of love for Him is the power that moves us in ministry:

> He died for all, that those who live might no longer live for themselves but for him who for their sake died and was raised. (2 Corinthians 5:15)

Paul continues by telling us that God's love controls us to the degree that the goals, values, and priorities of our lives are transformed. In the past we lived for ourselves, but now there has been a turning point, a breaking point, in our life experience. We no longer live for ourselves; now we live for Him who died and rose again on our behalf. He says it so simply and clearly! How could we continue to live for ourselves in the face of love so freely poured out? We have quit living for ourselves; now we live for Him:

> From now on, therefore, we regard no one according to the flesh. Even though we once regarded Christ according to the flesh, we regard him thus no longer. Therefore, if anyone is in Christ, he is a new creation. The old has passed away; behold, the new has come. (2 Corinthians 5:16-17)

Paul tells us now that this love that moves us, that transforms our goals, our values, and our priorities, also changes the way we see people. Paul says that from now on, we look at no one "according to the flesh." We look at no one from a worldly point of view. We are taught to see people from this world system's perspective. God wants to teach us to see people through His eyes.

This world has built into us a system of evaluation as a means of determining the value of people's lives. This system is so effective that we can actually spend ten minutes with other people and decide exactly what we think they are worth. We look at the color of their skin, the level of their education, the kind of house they live in, the car they drive, the kind of job they have, how much money they make, how much power and position they have attained. That is the way we discern the value of other people in this world.

When we come to the heart of this system of evaluation, however, we recognize that we are taught to look at people in terms of ways in which we can benefit from them. We learn to develop relationships with the wealthy so we can become wealthier. We know that by being friends with people in power, we can grow in power and authority. Often people are only objects to be used. That is the way we are taught to see people in the world around us. God will change our view of people as He motivates us by His love and as He transforms the priorities and values of our hearts. He will teach us to see people through His very own eyes. We will begin to look at them as new creations in Christ, and we will find their worth in the knowledge that they reflect the image of God, all their value through the eyes of the Father.

From the beginning of time God has called us to love people, and He gave us an abundance of things to be used in the process of serving them. Today the world teaches us to love things and to use people! Only when we see with God's eyes and respond with His heart will we be used of Him to give life to people.

The ministry of reconciliation God has entrusted to you and me will overflow as His love controls us, transforms our goals and priorities, and gives us the ability to see people through His eyes. This is the work of the Holy Spirit as He fills our eyes with the greatness of our God and moves us to His glorious purposes.

> All this is from God, who through Christ reconciled us to himself and gave us the ministry of reconciliation; that is, in Christ God was reconciling the world to himself, not counting their trespasses against them, and entrusting to us the message of reconciliation. (2 Corinthians 5:18-19)

If we have not experienced the divine process that Paul sets before us here, evangelism and missions will become merely programs in our churches. If our hearts are not gripped by Christ's love for us and our response love for Him, we will depend on pressure and manipulation as we seek to motivate God's people to pray, to give, and to go to those who have not yet heard the good news of Jesus. Only when our passions are owned by the God we serve will we be moved to lay down our lives for the gospel.

> Therefore, we are ambassadors for Christ, God making his appeal through us. We implore you on behalf of Christ, be reconciled to God. For our sake he made him to be sin who knew no sin, so that in him we might become the righteousness of God. (2 Corinthians 5:20-21)

Now God will miraculously open our eyes to see the eternal Kingdom that He is building in the midst of time and space!

A VISION OF HIS KINGDOM

In 2 Kings, we find Israel suffering a series of raids by the Arameans. As the king of Aram met with his officers to plan ambushes, God revealed those secrets to the prophet Elisha. Elisha, in turn, revealed to the king of Israel the enemy's battle plans. This so angered the king of Aram that he sought Elisha's capture. He sent soldiers by night to surround Elisha in the city of Dothan.

In the morning, Gehazi, Elisha's servant, was filled with fear when he saw that they were surrounded by the chariots and the horses of the enemy. He came and told Elisha, who said, "Don't be afraid, for those who are with us are more than those who are with them." I am sure Gehazi went out and took a second look. Still, all he could see were the chariots and horses of the enemy! Then,

> Elisha prayed and said, "O LORD, please open his eyes that he may see." So the LORD opened the eyes of the young man, and he saw, and behold, the mountain was full of horses and chariots of fire all around Elisha. (2 Kings 6:17)

Adequate!

The horses and chariots of fire were there the first time
Gehazi looked, but he could not see them with his physical eyes.
God must give us eyes to see what is eternal!

God is building a Kingdom that will last forever. There are two
kingdoms: the physical, temporal realm and the eternal Kingdom of God. God is building that Kingdom now in the realms of
time and space.

Our culture tells us that what is physical and material is the
basis of reality. This world is characterized by substance that can
be possessed and used. We may hope those things that deal with
the spiritual and eternal are true, but we can never be sure, so we
have to build our lives around what we know is real. All those
other things are shadows. This world is real; this is substance.

But God says, "No, it is the other way around!" It is this kingdom that is the world of shadows. His Kingdom is the realm of
substance. As we walk with God, He will open our eyes to see the
reality of His eternal Kingdom.

The Church of the Lord Jesus is the physical expression of
the Kingdom of God in this world. God will open our eyes to see
the value of His church the way He sees it. He will open our eyes
to see what He is doing in the lives of people around us. He will
open our eyes to the cities around us, to see the needs of hurting
people in their emptiness and their hopelessness. He will open
our eyes to see their desperate need for salvation, justice, and
hope.

God will open our eyes to see the church that He is building
around the world. He will give us a vision for that great day when
we will stand before Him with those from every tribe and tongue
and people and nation, and He will give us a heart for missions.
As we walk with God and He gives us that vision for the eternal
city He is building, He will do something wonderful in our hearts.
He will cause us to orient all our resources toward what is eter-

nal. Our time, our energy, our desires, and our finances will all be given to building what will last forever, not what will be consumed at the end of time. As this miraculous transformation takes place, the only thing worthy of the life of God—His Church—will now be worthy of our lives. God will bring us to the place where we will not spend our lives on anything less than that for which He spent His life. Our hearts and our resources will be consumed in God and in what He is doing, and we will lay down our lives for Christ and His Kingdom.

Many people today have chosen to create for themselves options for ministry other than the church. We have a proliferation of organizations, methods, structures, and procedures that have been developed to do the work of God "because the church just isn't doing it." This attitude is a great sin. Our vision can become so filled with who we are and what we are doing that we may fail to see what God is doing, the fact that only He can do it, and that He will do it only through His church. God has one purpose for the realm of time and space: to reveal Himself through His Son and to build an eternal body of believers who are mature in Christ, are filled with the knowledge of the Son of God, and who will glorify Him and enjoy Him forever. That Body is His Church, expressed in a multitude of local congregations throughout the world.

We have been called not only to see what God sees, but also to walk with Him in building His eternal Kingdom, as we serve Him as He leads in our own local church. There are many wonderful ministries that work alongside of and assist the Church of the Lord Jesus, contributing specialized work to the whole of the Body; however, we must remember that our ministries will have validity only to the degree that they are given to the building up of the Body of Christ.

All of this overflows from seeing God in His exalted greatness, holiness, and glory, and the vision of His greatness transforms us. He then enables us to see ourselves the way He sees us and to see people through His eyes. He opens our eyes to see the eternal Kingdom He is building, and He moves us by His love to walk with Him in its glorious fulfillment.

WHAT HAVE YOU SEEN?

In Exodus 33, we find Moses bringing before the Lord the boldest request in all of history. This came after the incident of the golden calf. It had been only three months since the children of Israel left Egypt. Moses had been up on the mountain for forty days communing with God. The intimacy of their relationship was growing, and Moses was developing an increasing hunger for God, a desire to see Him and to know Him. After forty days of being in God's presence, Moses surely would want to see more of God. But when he came down from the mountain, he saw instead the hard-hearted rebellion of God's people.

While Moses was on the mountain and God was writing the character of His heart on those tablets of stone, the people down in the valley were desiring other things. They wanted a god they could see with their eyes, like all the other nations around them possessed. Aaron, who had become Moses' mouthpiece, was leading them in the building of the golden calf. You might remember Aaron's explanation of the incident: "I said to them, 'Let any who have gold take it off.' So they gave it to me, and I threw it into the fire, and out came this calf" (Exodus 32:24). Moses was so angered! God had delivered His people from Egypt by the power of His hands, but now they were crying out and falling before this calf of gold.

> These are your gods, O Israel, who brought you up out of the land of Egypt! (Exodus 32:8b)

In his anger, Moses threw down the tablets of stone and destroyed them. God was so angered that He talked about withdrawing His presence from His people. Moses pleaded with God to not remove His presence; He could not go on if the Lord did not go with him. God assured Moses of His continuing presence, and in the intimacy of these moments, Moses asked God what is without question the boldest request any man has ever brought before the Lord:

Moses said, "Please show me your glory." (Exodus 33:18)

Moses asked to see God's glory! He had been communing with Him for forty days and desired Him more and more. God said, "Moses, you cannot see my face," but God met Moses at the point of his desire, and He revealed Himself to His servant.

He said, "I will make all my goodness pass before you and will proclaim before you my name 'The LORD.' And I will be gracious to whom I will be gracious, and will show mercy on whom I will show mercy. But," he said, "you cannot see my face, for man shall not see me and live." And the LORD said, "Behold, there is a place by me where you shall stand on the rock, and while my glory passes by I will put you in a cleft of the rock, and I will cover you with my hand until I have passed by. Then I will take away my hand, and you shall see my back, but my face shall not be seen." (Exodus 33:19-23)

We see such divine humility in the heart of our God. "Moses, there's a hollow place here in the rock. I'll put you there and cover you with my hand. After I pass by, I'll take my hand away, and you'll see my glory as I pass by." Moses asked to see God's glory, and God showed Moses the glory of His eternal name and the beauty of His compassionate heart. God revealed His goodness, His name, His grace, and His mercy. Who God is, what He is like, and how He gives Himself to people, are the vision of God that

Adequate!

Moses saw that day on the side of Mount Sinai. Moses hungered to see His glory, and God revealed His heart. God will stimulate within us a desire to see His face, and as we hunger for Him more and more, He will reveal His heart to us.

How do we see God's glory? We are shown the glory of God in the face of Jesus Christ. Jesus is the "exact representation of His being" (Hebrews 1:3, NIV). God revealed His heart to us in His Son. All of God's holiness, His compassion, His mercy, His righteousness, and His great heart of justice are revealed in His Son in a powerfully visual way. When God gives us eyes to see Jesus, we have seen the Father.

We have often done well knowing the mind of God in our churches today. We have not done as well knowing His heart. We have largely become a church that pursues insights, principles, and theological concepts. No other church in history has had sounder theology or has known as much about God as many of our churches do today. However, we seem to know so little about His heart. Maybe this has troubled you, too. With all our insight, all our knowledge, all our information, and all our depth of theology, we seem to have so much difficulty functioning in the most basic Christian things, like personal holiness and loving people more than things. In our churches we are so easily hurt, and we hold on to those hurts for so long. We easily walk away from one another and quickly leave our churches when we experience disappointments and failures. There is often much judging and little compassion. Too many people remain alone in their pain.

God desires to reveal His heart to us and to build His heart into us as we seek His face. Insight alone does not transform us; only the things that flow from the heart of God transform the lives of people. As God opens His heart to be known by us and as He builds His heart into us, His love will flow through us to those who are in desperate need of His forgiveness, His compassion, His healing, and His life.

For those of us who desire to be used of God, the time is long past for us to be saying to one another, "What do you know? Where have you been? What have you accomplished?" The time has come—if we desire to be used of God—to be saying to one another, "What have you seen of God? What do you know of Him?" To the degree that God gives us the grace to see Him, our lives and our ministries will become fruitful and effective. May God give us the grace to seek His face and to be transformed in His presence!

QUESTIONS FOR COMMUNICATION AND APPLICATION

1. How do you see God? How has that vision of God dealt with your inadequacies in ministry? When you think specifically of seeing His holiness, His glory, His power, His lordship, and His sovereignty, how has that affected your responses to Him and to ministry opportunities?

2. Are you willing to accept God's view of yourself? In what ways do you tend to see yourself or your abilities as more than God does? as less?

3. How has God taught you to see people the same way He sees people? Do you see God's own characteristics, such as love, patience, or anger expressed in your own responses to people?

4. What is the degree of your commitment to the Kingdom that God is building? Do you see yourself giving your resources of time, energy, and gifts to build lesser things? How does God want you to respond to that?

I perceived that whatever God does endures forever; nothing can be added to it, nor anything taken from it. God has done it, so that people fear before him. That which is, already has been; that which is to be, already has been; and God seeks what has been driven away.

Ecclesiastes 3:14-15

2
A Responsive Heart

The character and nature of God's work in this world are unmistakable. It is His alone. What God does can never be duplicated by man; it is always marked uniquely by His eternal attributes. It is a great blow to our pride to realize that only God can do His work, but at the same time, this understanding can free us to live as God has designed us: as responsive servants who trust in a sovereign God to do His will.

At seventeen years of age, just before my senior year in high school, I became a Christian; I was very immature as a person and stayed immature as a Christian for a very long time. I am still hoping that someday I am going to be able to take something other than "baby steps" in my walk with the Lord. Not long after I became a Christian, I became involved in a youth ministry and continued to work with that organization throughout my studies in college and seminary. We provided social activities for young people, planned many evangelistic outreaches, and had a wonderful time. If anyone had come to me during those years and said, "What is it that makes ministry effective?" I would have answered in all sincerity, "A good education, a good personality, good tools to work with." I had not yet learned that ministry is what God does.

I vividly remember a retreat we conducted for the staff of that organization. I can still picture myself walking by the shore of the lake where we were meeting, talking with Terry, my closest friend and longtime co-worker. As we walked along, he said, "You know, Bill, we don't have a ministry."

"What do you mean we don't have a ministry—look at everything we are doing," I replied. "Look at all the response we're having, all the good experiences. What do you mean we don't have a ministry?"

"We don't have a ministry," Terry reaffirmed. "There is nothing unique that God has done in our hearts or that He is doing in people through us; we are just duplicating what we see other people doing—just manufacturing activity."

My friend's words were devastating to me. However, as I look back at that experience by the lake, I see it as a real turning point in my life and ministry—it was a time when I began to seek God for what He would do in and through me.

There is only one answer to the question "What makes ministry effective?" The answer is God! If ministry is what God does, then the key to an effective ministry must be found in seeking Him.

ASK WHAT I SHALL GIVE YOU

In 2 Chronicles, we find the time God said to Solomon, "Ask for whatever you want me to give you." As far as we know, no one else in history has had that same offer from the Lord in just that way.

In that night God appeared to Solomon, and said to him, "Ask what I shall give you." And Solomon said to God, "You have shown great and steadfast love to David my father, and have made me king in his place. O LORD God, let your word to David my father be now fulfilled, for you have made me king over a people as numerous as the dust of the earth. Give me now wisdom and knowledge to go out and come in before this people, for who can govern this people of yours, which is so great?" (2 Chronicles 1:7-10)

God was pleased with Solomon's choice. Rather than seek those things that would make his own life luxurious and powerful, Solomon sought that which would most benefit His people. In His great mercy, God also gave Solomon the riches and honor that he did not request:

God answered Solomon, "Because this was in your heart, and you have not asked possessions, wealth, honor, or the life of those who hate you, and have not even asked long life, but have asked wisdom and knowledge for yourself that you may govern my people over whom I have made you king, wisdom and knowledge are granted to you. I will also give you riches, possessions, and honor, such as none of the kings had who were before you, and none after you shall have the like." (2 Chronicles 1:11-12)

Though there is no record in the Scriptures that God ever came to Solomon's father, David, with this same offer, in Psalm 27 we seem to see the response of David's heart to this same question: "Ask what I should give you."

One thing have I asked of the LORD, that will I seek after: that I may dwell in the house of the LORD all the days of my life, to gaze upon the beauty of the LORD and to inquire in his temple....Hear, O LORD, when I cry aloud; be gracious to me and answer me! You have said, "Seek my face." My heart says to you, "Your face, LORD, do I seek." (Psalm 27:4, 7-8)

Solomon asked for wisdom; David asked for God Himself. God was pleased with Solomon's choice; it was a good choice, and we must take nothing from that. At the same time, we must say that anytime we ask for less than God, we are asking for less than what God desires to give to us. We see the fruit of these two men's choices in their life experiences. David, even in his great weakness, failure, and sin, possessed a heart that moved closer and closer to God. God kept calling him, and David kept responding with a whole heart. The longer David lived, the more responsive to God David's heart grew. Solomon, even with all his wisdom, became filled with cynicism and emptiness toward the end of his life.

WISDOM, MADNESS, AND FOLLY

We find in the book of Ecclesiastes some of the most interesting truths in all the Word of God. The Scriptures are very revealing about Solomon's life and the state of his heart. Even with all his wisdom, Solomon is struggling deeply as he evaluates his life and his work:

> The words of the Preacher, the son of David, king in Jerusalem. Vanity of vanities, says the Preacher, vanity of vanities! All is vanity. (Ecclesiastes 1:1-2)

Solomon hardly begins the book when the cynicism begins to pour out of his heart! "Vanity of vanities...All is vanity!" Nothing seems to make a difference. Then he asks a key question:

> What does man gain by all the toil at which he toils under the sun? (Ecclesiastes 1:3)

What is it that comes back to a man as a result of the work he does? Is there any satisfaction, any real joy, any fulfillment or sense of completion?

> A generation goes, and a generation comes, but the earth remains forever. (Ecclesiastes 1:4)

Whatever great contributions have been made, whatever significant accomplishments on the part of generation after generation, the earth continues on the course God has prepared for it:

> I have seen everything that is done under the sun, and behold, all is vanity and a striving after wind. What is crooked cannot be made straight, and what is lacking cannot be counted. (Ecclesiastes 1:14-15)

Solomon has a sense that even with the vast wisdom God has entrusted to him, he is limited in what he can contribute. There seems to be a frustration that he cannot really make a difference in those places where a difference must be made.

Going into chapter 2, Solomon talks about the variety of ways in which he sought fulfillment in his life. He talks about pleasures and about laughter. He cheered himself with wine and then embraced folly. He talks about undertaking great projects. He made gardens and parks, reservoirs of water, and groves of flourishing trees. He bought male and female slaves. He amassed silver and gold. In every way possible, Solomon sought to fill up his life. Of course, King Solomon had a lot more avenues with which to seek fulfillment than most of us have, but he says,

> I turned to consider wisdom and madness and folly. For what can the man do who comes after the king? Only what has already been done. Then I saw that there is more gain in wisdom than in folly, as there is more gain in light than in darkness. (Ecclesiastes 2:12-13)

Solomon's work was so complete, his kingdom so beautiful and fruitful, his accomplishments so overwhelming, that he honestly asked the question, "What can the man do who comes after me; I have already done it all!" There has never been a kingdom like Solomon's with its beauty, the wisdom with which it was ruled, the riches, the gold, the silver, the glory, the political alliances. Yet in spite of Solomon's wisdom and accomplishments, Solomon's heart seems to have remained empty and unfulfilled:

> Of the wise as of the fool there is no enduring remembrance, seeing that in the days to come all will have been long forgotten. How the wise dies just like the fool! So I hated life, because what is done under the sun was grievous to me, for all is vanity and a striving after wind. I hated all my toil in which I toil under the sun, seeing that I must leave it to the man who will come after me, and who knows whether he will be wise or a fool? Yet he will be master of all for which I toiled and used my wisdom under the sun. This also is vanity. So I turned about and gave my heart up to despair over all the toil of my labors under the sun. (Ecclesiastes 2:16-20)

This is the place in which Solomon finds himself. He hates life; he hates all the things he has toiled for. He completely despairs over everything that he has done. He knows that he is going to be leaving the scene before too long. His life is reaching its end, and someone else is going to take his place. Who knows whether he will be a wise man or a fool? Yet he will have charge of everything that Solomon has done. Surely the man that followed Solomon would not have the wisdom with which he was uniquely blessed. He may even be a complete fool, but he will have charge over all of Solomon's work. We can sense the frustration in Solomon's heart. Everything he has accomplished might not last for even one more generation.

ETERNITY IN THEIR HEARTS

In chapter 3, we see the beautiful Scripture text about the appropriateness of everything in its time. God always acts in the fullness of time. In His sovereign timing, He does what pleases Him. In verse 9, Solomon again asks the key question:

What gain has the worker from his toil? (Ecclesiastes 3:9)

What comes back to a man as the result of his work? Is there any sense of joy, of completion, or fulfillment?

I have seen the business that God has given to the children of man to be busy with. (Ecclesiastes 3:10)

Other translations give this as, "I have seen the tasks that God has assigned to men" (NASB). Solomon's perspective is beginning to change a little bit. Up to this point he has been talking about the overwhelming significance of everything he has done, all the greatness of his accomplishments. Now he begins to talk about burdens that God lays on men or tasks that He assigns to them.

When we refer to "tasks," we are not referring to overwhelming accomplishments, are we? A task is what we assign to our children when they come home from school to occupy them until supper time. Solomon is beginning to gain a better perspective of how God fulfills His purposes. What God is doing is not dependent on the overwhelmingly significant things we do. A more realistic perspective is that for all people, God assigns each one a task to occupy them while they are here; then God puts all those tasks together into an eternally significant work!

He has made everything beautiful in its time. Also, he has put eternity into man's heart, yet so that he cannot find out what God has done from the beginning to the end. (Ecclesiastes 3:11)

The man that God has created to live in time has been blessed with an eternal perspective. God has set "eternity in our hearts"! We are unique among all God's creatures, because we can see life from an eternal point of view.

I perceived that there is nothing better for them than to be joyful and to do good as long as they live; also that everyone should eat and drink and take pleasure in all his toil—this is God's gift to man. (Ecclesiastes 3:12-13)

Solomon tells us now that what we really ought to do is eat, drink, be merry, and enjoy our work. This almost sounds like an existentialist speaking, doesn't it? The existentialist says that the past is completely irrelevant and the future is completely uncertain. What we ought to do is try to fill up our lives right now in whatever way pleases us. Eat, drink, and be merry, for tomorrow we may die! Solomon is coming from a different perspective, however. He is talking about how God sovereignly does what pleases Him and how that understanding sets us free to enjoy our lives and our work. This truth removes the pressure to "accomplish great things" and allows us to rest in God as we walk with Him. Solomon now sets before us an insight that must grip our hearts.

WHAT GOD DOES WILL REMAIN FOREVER

I perceived that whatever God does endures forever. (Ecclesiastes 3:14a)

Solomon is frustrated, knowing that his kingdom might not last for even one more generation. As God is expanding Solomon's mind and heart, and as he sees more clearly from an eternal perspective, he says: "I know that everything God does will remain forever." What God touches lasts for eternity, and the great king now builds even further on this truth.

Nothing can be added to it, nor anything taken from it. God has done it, so that people fear before him. (Ecclesiastes 3:14b)

What God does will never fade away. No man, no matter how intelligent or gifted he is, no matter how spiritual, can ever add anything to what God is doing. No one, no matter how significant or powerful or even how evil he is, can take anything away from what God is doing. God wants us to understand how powerfully and completely He holds sovereign control over the universe. We stand in awe, reverence, and worship before Him. Although God greatly desires us to be involved with Him in His eternal work, He is dependent on us for nothing. In His mercy, He calls us to walk with Him as He builds His Church, but God does not need us!

Who are the most spiritual men and women you think of as you look back over history? Do you think of Abraham, Enoch, Moses, David, or Paul? Do you think of Mary or Mother Theresa? Do you think of the great church fathers, or of the great missionary statesmen throughout history? Not one of them has added one thing to what God is doing! Who are the most evil men you can think of in history? Do you think of Pharaoh, Nero, Hitler, or Stalin? Not one of them has subtracted one iota from what God is doing.

Are you sensing with me what this great truth teaches us? It tells us that the day when Martin Luther walked up the steps and nailed those 95 theses on the church door, God did not breathe a sigh of relief. He did not say, "At last, someone understands what the Church is all about! Maybe my plan will be fulfilled after all." It also tells us that when Nero took God's elect and dipped them in oil or tar and used them as torches to light his gardens at night, God was not one bit fearful about His ability to fulfill His will. No one can add anything to what God is doing; no one can take anything from it. God has designed His work in that way so we stand in awe, wonder, and worship before Him. When time merges with eternity again, everything that was in the heart of God to be done in time will have been accomplished. There will be no loose ends. Nothing will be left undone, and God will be the only explanation for its fulfillment. That is why God will be worshiped for all eternity by all His creatures.

SEEKING WHAT HAS PASSED BY

> That which is, already has been; that which is to be, already has been; and God seeks what has been driven away. (Ecclesiastes 3:15)

What is, has already been. Look around you; what do you see? It has already been there. I remember watching a television program with my sons on the world of the telescope and the world of the microscope. Through the power of the electronic microscope, on a piece of dust or a drop of water entire worlds could be seen! In contrast, through a powerful telescope the far reaches of the solar system could be seen. How do we respond when we discover those wonderful things that have been hidden for centuries? Do we worship the Creator who made them? No, we worship the creature who discovers them! God says, "Look around you at what is there. It has already been." God has been glorified for millennia in the existence of these things, and we did not even know they existed!

God then states, "What will be, has already been also." A few years ago, my wife's grandfather died at the age of ninety-eight. I sat down with the family after the funeral and we talked about the fact that as a little boy, he would get up at first light and hitch the horses to the plow—then he lived to see men walk on the moon! What do you think is going to happen in the next hundred years if our Lord does not return first? We cannot even begin to imagine these things. We do know, however, that whatever great things we accomplish as a people, they will not cause us as humanity to worship the Creator who brought them into existence. We worship the creatures who achieve them. God says, "What *will* be—that has already been, too."

Not only has what is there already been there, but also what will be has already been! "God will call the past into account" (Ecclesiastes 3:15, NIV), or "God seeks what has passed by" (NASB). This is an amazing statement! God is talking here of the relationship between time and eternity. He is not looking for new things to happen in time; He is looking for old things to happen in time.

Some years ago my brother-in-law was attending a Sunday school class in which the teacher was discussing time. After he asked, "What is time?" one student immediately put up his hand and said, "Time is what keeps everything from happening at the same time." That is an amazing response right off the top of someone's head! What is time? Time is the realm in which God works out physically what has already taken place in His mind and heart in eternity. God is not seeking new things to take place in time; rather He is seeking old things to be worked out in time.

We have many pictures of this great truth in Scripture. Do you remember how the writer to the Hebrews describes the instructions God gave Moses for building the Tabernacle?

> *They serve a copy and shadow of the heavenly things.* For when Moses was about to erect the tent, he was instructed by God, saying, "See that you make everything according to the pattern that was shown you on the mountain." (Hebrews 8:5, emphasis added)

The Tabernacle Moses built was a copy of the reality that exists in the heavenlies! This is a picture of the relationship between time and eternity. Time is a reflection of eternity and a realm in which our Father fulfills physically the desires of His heart.

The Scriptures tell us that Christ was slain before the foundation of the world (Revelation 13:8). We know that in time, Christ died in A.D. 30. on Mt. Calvary in Jerusalem. That is the place in which God's plan was worked out physically, but in fact, in the heart of our Father, the Son was slain before the worlds began! The Scriptures tell us that you and I were chosen in Christ before the foundation of the world (Ephesians 1:4). Here we are, living in the twenty-first century, but God knew us as persons before He created the heavens and the earth. Some of us, who remember when we began to follow Christ, might say, "I know when I chose to believe in Christ. It was my decision." But in fact, our decision was a response to the purposes centered in the heart of our Father from eternity. He knew us, and He chose us to belong to Him. That is why we know Christ; that is why we are children of God. In His purposes, time is a realm in which He works out physically those things that have already taken place in His mind and in His heart. If our hearts can take hold of what Solomon is teaching us in these verses, we and our ministries will be transformed.

A VESSEL FOR THE FATHER'S LIFE

I would like to lay some scriptural pictures over these great truths that God is teaching us through King Solomon. We see both the Lord Jesus and the apostle Paul walking in full understanding of God as the source and fulfillment of all His works. In John's Gospel, Jesus talked about the work of the Father, and the Pharisees were offended by His allusion to the work of the Father and His placing Himself on an equal plane with God:

> Jesus said to them, "Truly, truly, I say to you, the Son can do nothing of his own accord, but only what he sees the Father doing. For whatever the Father does, that the Son does likewise. For the Father loves the Son and shows him all that he himself is doing. And greater works than these will he show him, so that you may marvel. (John 5:19-20)

The Son can do nothing of Himself. That is an amazing statement! Jesus is God, but He tells us here that He can do nothing but what He sees the Father doing. Then the Son does what He sees the Father doing. This great theme comes up again and again in John's Gospel. Jesus continually describes the Father as the initiative in His life and ministry and in Jesus' response to His Father. Nothing ever began with Jesus. Again and again we hear Him say that the words He is speaking are the words of His Father. The works He is doing are the works of His Father. Jesus is a vessel through whom God is speaking His words and accomplishing His works that will last through all eternity. Jesus walked in that way because He knew what Solomon was teaching us: Only what God does will endure forever! Jesus limited His life and His ministry to the eternal works of the Father through Him. What the Son saw the Father doing is what the Son did in like manner.

We see two incredible assumptions in this portion of Scripture. First, we see no pressure on the part of the Lord Jesus to figure out what the Father was doing. He was confident that the Father would show Him. We see in Jesus' ministry an "apparent spontaneity" that allowed Him to move and respond to people, needs, and circumstances as the Spirit led Him. We have that same freedom and confidence because we have the Holy Spirit, and He will show us what the Father is doing so that we can participate with Him.

The second amazing assumption is that whatever the Father is doing is what the Son ought to do. Isn't it interesting that the apostle John did not say: "The Father loves the Son and shows Him everything He wants the Son to do." When the Father shows the Son what He is doing, the Son will do likewise. We, too, can live with the confidence that God will show us what He is doing by His Word and His Spirit, and that we have the joy of joining with Him in His work.

What do you see the Father doing? What do you see God doing in your life, your marriage, your family, your neighborhood, your church? If we did only what we saw the Father doing, how would that affect our ministries? When we come together as leaders of the church, how often do we spend our time talking about *our* plans, *our* visions, *our* goals, and *our* dreams? What if we did only what we saw the Father doing? What do we see the Father doing in our midst? Do we ever ask the question as we meet together as boards, committees, and congregations?

A few years ago I was involved in a new church ministry in which the pastor was Pat Dillon, one of my closest friends. Pat had gone to Stanford University as an atheist. While he was there, God grabbed his heart and transformed his life. He then grew as a Christian under the ministry and discipleship of Ray Stedman, former pastor of Peninsula Bible Church in Palo Alto, California.

During the time we were beginning this new church, Pat and I had the opportunity to go to California for a conference. As a couple of guys beginning a church and filled with dreams, we called Ray and asked if we could have lunch with him, because we had some questions that we wanted this great man of God to answer. One burning question was, "How do you stimulate within someone a hunger for God—a desire for the Scriptures?" I will never forget Ray's answer: "You can't do that," he replied. "There is nothing you can do to stimulate within anyone a hunger for God or a desire for His Word. All you can do is teach the Scriptures and keep your eyes wide open to see in whose life God is working. When you see God working, you jump in there as fast as you can and start fanning the flame. But only God can create a desire for Himself."

What do we see God doing? So often our eyes are so filled with all that we desire to do that we have no sense at all what God is doing. Jesus watched to see what God was doing, and that is what He did.

We see this same theme in John 8:

Jesus said to them, "When you have lifted up the Son of Man, then you will know that I am he, and that I do nothing on my own authority, but speak just as the Father taught me. And he who sent me is with me. He has not left me alone, for I always do the things that are pleasing to him." (John 8:28-29)

There was a consuming desire in the heart of the Son of God to do those things that pleased His Father. How did Jesus plan His ministry? How did He walk from day to day? Did He get up in the morning and say to His disciples, "What do you think we should do today? Should we go over to Samaria and talk to a woman at a well? Or should we go over to Capernaum and work some miracles there and see if anyone there will believe? It's a nice day today, and we don't know how much longer the weather is going to hold. Why don't we go down to the sea of Galilee and hold a service?" No.

"That is not how my ministry happens," Jesus told His disciples. "It all starts with the Father. Nothing starts in my mind or heart; it begins in the heart of the Father and works out through me. I do nothing on my own."

Jesus Christ was undoubtedly the most resourceful, insightful, and capable person ever to walk this earth. Although He never ceased to be deity, He willfully limited His own words and actions to those of His Father. Christ described His own life and ministry as an expression of His Father's words and works:

Do you not believe that I am in the Father and the Father is in me? The words that I say to you I do not speak on my own authority, but the Father who dwells in me does his works. (John 14:10)

Jesus was a vessel for the words and works of His Father; He understood what Solomon was talking about. No one can add

67

anything to what God is doing, and no one can take anything away from what God is doing. God has designed His works that way so that we stand in awe before Him and worship Him. What is there, has already been. What will be, has already been also! God seeks what has passed by and calls the past into account. Jesus knew that only what God does will endure forever. He knew that God desired to do His eternal works through His Son, so He came to His Father with a responsive heart, seeking His Father's initiative and power. Then God spoke His words and did His work. This is our model for ministry if we would be used of God.

A Shared Life Relationship

There is a strong relationship between John 14 and John 15. Jesus had said to His disciples in John 14:10: "The Father living in me is doing His work" (paraphrased). That is Jesus' explanation for His life and His ministry. As you well know, He will say to His disciples in the beginning of John 15, "My life abiding in you does my work" (paraphrased).

> I am the true vine, and my Father is the vinedresser. Every branch of mine that does not bear fruit he takes away, and every branch that does bear fruit he prunes, that it may bear more fruit. Already you are clean because of the word that I have spoken to you. (John 15:1-3)

Isn't this an amazing statement? Jesus has not yet been to the cross, He has not yet shed His blood, and yet He says to His disciples, "You are already clean." What do you think Jesus was trying to accomplish with His disciples in those years they walked together? Do you think He was giving them a theological system or code of ethics, or was He preparing them for the great work of building the Church? Of course, it was some of that, but primarily He was cleansing their lives day by day by the words He spoke! We need a far greater vision for the cleansing power of the Word of God in our lives and in the lives of the people God has entrusted to us.

> Abide in me, and I in you. As the branch cannot bear fruit by itself, unless it abides in the vine, neither can you, unless you abide in me. I am the vine; you are the branches. Whoever abides in me and I in him, he it is that bears much fruit, for apart from me you can do nothing. (John 15:4-5)

These words are devastating to us if we have any sense of pride. "Apart from me you can do nothing at all." Jesus' teachings crush our self confidence! We are trained people with excellent educations. We have worked hard to develop ourselves; we are resource people. That is the way of this world. We develop ourselves to the highest place possible, and then we go out and sell ourselves to the highest bidder. Many of us have vast experiences and many accomplishments. Now God says to us, "Apart from me you can do nothing at all."

What does Jesus mean by this? Does He mean, "Apart from me you cannot achieve the righteousness God demands in your life?" Surely He must mean that. Does He mean, "Apart from me you cannot live a good, moral life in this world?" He must mean that, too. Does He mean, "Apart from me you cannot love your wife or your husband or your children?" Does He mean, "Apart from me you cannot get up in the morning and do the job you do every day?" Does He mean, "Apart from me you cannot come home from work and do your normal household chores?" How far does this go? Where is the dividing line between the things we can handle pretty well on our own and the things we cannot do without God's help? There is no dividing line, is there? Apart from Him we can do nothing! The truth is that every breath we take—even for those who curse God—we take only as a result of His grace.

This truth is devastating to our pride, yes, but it can also be the beginning point for a fruitful ministry. Apart from Him we can do nothing at all. Jesus has been modeling these truths for us in His own life and ministry as revealed in the Gospels. We see in His relationship with His Father a responsive heart that seeks God. He is a vessel through whom God speaks, a vessel through which God does His work. Jesus knew that only what God does will remain forever. Everything else will come to nothing.

In this great passage on the vine and the branches, Jesus is calling His disciples to fruitfulness. They desire to be used of Him, but I think they were experiencing some pressure concerning the fruit. We are like that; we want God to use us; we have hearts that desire Him and pursue His glory. But sometimes in real life ministry situations, we feel the pressure to "produce." Jesus is telling His disciples, and you and me, that nothing in us can result in the fruitfulness that comes only from the heart of God. Therefore, we must cease striving, stop trying to produce "ministry." Jesus is calling us to take our focus off the fruit and place it on our relationship with Him. He tells us that if we share His life and let Him share our lives, everything that we both desire will flow out of us in abundance.

Isn't it amazing that Jesus does not tell us how to "abide in Him"? He does not say, "Have your devotions every morning." He does not say, "Go to church three times a week; memorize Scripture." He does not give us a formula, but He does say, "Come to me and share my life. Let me share your life. Everything we both desire will flow in abundance out of that shared life relationship." Devotions are valuable; church attendance is critical; memorizing Scripture is helpful. However, our fruitfulness will not flow out of our performances; it will flow out of our relationship with

God. Our focus must be knowing God, seeking Him, being changed by Him day by day, and God will do His eternal works through us.

The "big picture" that we see, Solomon's teaching in Ecclesiastes 3, is powerfully transforming. No one can add anything to what God is doing, and no one can take anything from it. This truth leads us to worship. God seeks what has passed by, and time becomes a reflection of eternity, that realm in which God works out physically what has already taken place in His mind and heart. Jesus modeled this truth and then called His disciples to walk with Him in that same way. Now His life abiding in us will fulfill His works. A wonderful verse in the book of Ephesians talks about this very truth:

> We are his workmanship, created in Christ Jesus for good works, which God prepared beforehand, that we should walk in them. (Ephesians 2:10)

God has called us to walk in the works He has prepared for us from all eternity. We come before the Lord with a responsive heart, abiding, sharing the life of the Father through the Son. He then pours His life through us in the fulfillment of His will.

LED FORTH IN TRIUMPH

We find one of the most exciting verses in the Bible in 2 Corinthians 2:

> Thanks be to God, who in Christ always leads us in triumphal procession, and through us spreads the fragrance of the knowledge of him everywhere. (2 Corinthians 2:14)

God always triumphs; He never ever fails. And He has called us to participate with Him in His triumph. Satan, the father of lies, would love to convince us that when we fail, God fails. No,

Adequate!

God never fails. God always triumphs. His Son is the means by which He triumphs, and He has called us to walk with Him in a triumphal procession through all time and history.

A few years ago I was invited for the first time to Colombia for a time of ministry. When I arrived at the airport in Bogotá, no one was there to meet me. I have arrived at a number of airports where there was no one to meet me, but Bogotá was different—I was in a foreign country! I finally got all my stuff together and was standing alone in front of the airport at nine at night. I could not even remember the word *amigo* to tell the policeman who was patrolling the area that a friend was coming to meet me! I was sitting on top of my suitcases and my boxes in that foreign city feeling very lonely and depressed. About midnight, after the policeman had walked past me three or four times, he tried to help me. I could not even make a phone call. I had no pesos and did not know how to use the telephones. After we searched through my correspondence, he made some phone calls. I then learned that because I was going to be working with two different mission groups, each had thought the other was coming to meet me.

About 1:00 a.m. I finally arrived at the group house of Wycliffe Bible Translators in Bogotá. As I lay in bed, staring at the ceiling and trying to calm down from the events of the day, I realized it was from this very place just a few months earlier that the leftists had taken Chet Bitterman captive. They had been looking for the director of the work, but he was occupied in the ministry at another place. They took Chet instead and held him captive. They said to Wycliffe, "Either you get out of Colombia, or we'll kill him." Wycliffe knew that if they submitted to that threat, the leftists would then pick the next most visible ministry, kidnap one of its people, and say, "Now *you* get out." Wycliffe, with its ministry among the Indian tribes in the jungle areas, was perceived to be a real threat by the Communist leaders. They held Chet captive, and the leaders in Wycliffe endured. It seems as if the leftists had developed a real affection for Chet but felt they had painted themselves into a corner. After 87 days they shot Chet through the heart and left his body on a bus in Bogotá.

When I was at the translation center in Lomalinda, Colombia, I was visiting with a friend who was working on the illustrations for a book on Chet's life. He began telling me about some of the things that were going on between the Communists and Chet. As his captors were developing an openness toward Chet, they allowed him to write to his wife, Brenda. They would pass the letters back and forth, and Chet's letters were filled with Scripture offering hope to his wife and expressing confidence in God. As the leftists were passing these letters back and forth, somehow they were "leaked" to the newspapers. Some of the newspapers began to print Chet's letters to Brenda; however, they printed not only the Scripture references but also the Scripture verses! Here were Communist-leaning newspapers filled with page after page of the Scriptures!

Nothing in recent years has backfired on the leftists in Colombia as powerfully as the incident with Chet Bitterman. God has used it so effectively to raise an interest in the gospel and to call others to service in Chet's place. Many people have gone to the mission field because of his witness. I had the privilege of teaching some years later at the Wycliffe translation center in Papua New Guinea. There I met Chet's widow, Brenda, who was serving the Lord in that wonderful base for ministry. Visiting with her and looking into her face, I knew that Satan had no victory in this entire incident.

When one walks down to the little cemetery at Lomalinda, Colombia, where Chet is buried, and looks at Chet's headstone, this verse is visible: "Thanks be to God who always leads us in triumphal procession in Christ and through us spreads everywhere

Adequate!

the fragrance of the knowledge of Him" (2 Corinthians 2:14, NIV). God never fails; He always triumphs. The enemies of the gospel had no victory in Colombia:

> We are the aroma of Christ to God among those who are being saved and among those who are perishing, to one a fragrance from death to death, to the other a fragrance from life to life. Who is sufficient for these things? (2 Corinthians 2:15-16)

I think as Paul is writing, he is visualizing the great armies of the Roman Empire. They would go out from Rome, seeking to conquer the surrounding cities and nations. After the battles they would come back in a triumphal procession. First would come the most senior officers, then other officers, and then some enlisted men. Following them would be those who were taken captive in the battles—some to die in the arena, others to be slaves. Finally would come the rest of the soldiers. As the conquerors marched through the cities and towns on its way back to Rome, people would run out to meet them and throw flower petals in their path. As the soldiers and the captives walked over and crushed those petals, the aroma would be released. To those who were returning triumphant, this was the aroma of life; but to those who were going to die in the arena or to live as slaves, this was the stench of death.

That is a picture of what we are experiencing in ministry. To those who are responding to the life of God within us, we are the aroma of life; to those who hate and despise Him, we are the aroma of death. This is a wonderful picture of ministry—the overflow of God's life through us as we walk responsively with Him. Paul closes the verse with the question that confronts all of us who would be used of God: "Who is sufficient for these things?" Whenever we face opportunities for ministry, the question of adequacy raises its ugly head. Who is adequate for this? Before Paul comes back to this question, he begins to speak of his integrity as a servant of the Lord.

> We are not, like so many, peddlers of God's word, but as men of sincerity, as commissioned by God, in the sight of God we speak in Christ. Are we beginning to commend ourselves again? Or do we need, as some do, letters of recommendation to you, or from you? You yourselves are our letter of recommendation, written on our hearts, to be known and read by all. And you show that you are a letter from Christ delivered by us, written not with ink but with the Spirit of the living God, not on tablets of stone but on tablets of human hearts. (2 Corinthians 2:17-3:3)

We know that the Corinthian church had some real difficulty with the apostle Paul. He had written them some very confrontational letters about their confusion and fleshly attitudes in the use of spiritual gifts. He dealt with their competition and the party spirit that existed among them. He confronted them about allowing a man to live in sin with his stepmother. Of all the churches in which Paul had ministered, the church at Corinth struggled most in their hearts toward him.

We can almost sense their attitudes reflected in Paul's words to them here. It is as if they had said to Paul, "Next time you come to visit us or you send a letter, why don't you have one of the 'real apostles' write a letter of recommendation for you saying Paul is a real apostle, he docs have authority in your lives, and you need to listen to him." This is Paul's response: "You are our letter! Look at your lives. Look at your church. Are you the same people that you were before God brought us to you? Of course not. That is the evidence of our ministry and of my apostleship."

Where does our competence come from? Is there any degree we can point to on a wall, a diploma, any accreditation from men that qualifies us for ministry? As valuable as those things are, the only thing that qualifies us for ministry is that God has done something in our hearts through His Son, and by His Spirit God is doing something through us in the lives of others. That is where our authority comes from. The fruit of God's life is evident through us, in the lives of those whom we are serving.

A NEW COVENANT

In 2 Corinthians 3, Paul begins to contrast the old and the new covenants. He talks about the one written with ink and the other with the Spirit of the living God, one on tablets of stone and the other on human hearts. One has its source in this world, the other its source in the heart of a Holy God. One is written on tablets of stone that will last for all time, but the other on hearts that will last for eternity. In verse 7 he speaks of the ministry of death and the ministry of life, how one covenant has glory that fades and the other has glory that lasts. One condemns, and the other brings righteousness.

> If the ministry of death, carved in letters on stone, came with such glory that the Israelites could not gaze at Moses' face because of its glory, which was being brought to an end, will not the ministry of the Spirit have even more glory? For if there was glory in the ministry of condemnation, the ministry of righteousness must far exceed it in glory. Indeed, in this case, what once had glory has come to have no glory at all, because of the glory that surpasses it. (2 Corinthians 3:7-10)

The characteristics of God's life touching the lives of people cannot be duplicated in any way. Ministry that changes hearts and produces glory and righteousness that never fade away is God's alone.

Paul is contrasting the old and the new covenants. The old covenant is the covenant of the law. Jesus brought us into a new covenant relationship with the Father. As you remember, on the last night Jesus spent with His disciples before going to the cross, He shared the last supper with them.

> Likewise the cup after they had eaten, saying, "This cup that is poured out for you is the new covenant in my blood." (Luke 22:20)

Jesus is introducing a completely new relationship with the Father to all who will place their trust in Him. This is a relationship of life, freedom, intimacy, and power. Paul describes the heart of that new covenant relationship in this way:

> Such is the confidence that we have through Christ toward God. Not that we are sufficient in ourselves to claim anything as coming from us, but our sufficiency is from God, who has made us competent to be ministers of a new covenant, not of the letter but of the Spirit. For the letter kills, but the Spirit gives life. (2 Corinthians 3:4-6)

The question of adequacy is dealt with here! We are not adequate or sufficient in ourselves to consider anything as coming from us. Our adequacy comes from God! Our resources come from Him. Our confidence comes from Him. He makes us competent, or adequate, as servants of a new covenant. In the "old covenant" relationship with God, before we knew Him by faith, the resources for our lives came from us. In Satan's temptation, Adam and Eve became convinced they could be gods themselves. They turned inward toward themselves, placing their confidence in who *they* were and what *they* could accomplish. God allowed them to do this, then gave humankind the law, His righteous standard for the way we ought to live. However, God was not going to give us any help to keep the old covenant. He wanted us to understand our helplessness, our hopelessness, in the face of His law.

Adequate!

In the old covenant relationship with God, before we came to know Christ, all the resources for our lives came from ourselves. Paul is teaching us in the new covenant relationship we share with God through His Son, that all our adequacy, our sufficiency, our power, and our resources come from Him.

This truth is difficult for us to grasp. For years we have learned to depend on ourselves. We face temptations, and we want to "gut it out." We face opportunities to witness, and we want to depend on our ability to remember all the right verses, to move people with our persuasiveness. We have teaching opportunities, and we tend to trust in our ideas and our eloquence. We see hurting people, and we lean on our compassion and resources. In a new-covenant ministry, all the resources for life and ministry no longer come from us; they come from God.

We need to learn in every ministry situation to say, "God, I am not capable for this; I am not adequate; I am not sufficient. I have nothing to say here that will make any difference. I cannot persuade these people; I cannot move them in the right direction. Unless You do this, it will not happen." We seek God for what He will do. When we face a difficulty in a relationship, we must seek God for His healing power and His love—there is nothing that comes from us that will make it right. As we share our faith with others, we must place our hope in a God who draws people to Himself rather than in our ability to convince them. We turn continually to God for what He will do rather than trust in ourselves. This is the way God has called us to live from the very beginning of time. This is the relationship with God that brings fruitfulness in ministry.

Paul taught this same truth to the church at Colossae when he told them of God's mystery that was now being revealed through His Church.

To them God chose to make known how great among the Gentiles are the riches of the glory of this mystery, which is Christ in you, the hope of glory. (Colossians 1:27)

The key to life and ministry is not who we are; it is not what we are able to do. Who Christ is and what He is able to do in us and through us is our only hope in life, in ministry, and in relationships.

ANY BUSH WILL DO

We talked about God's call to Moses earlier. Moses was walking in the wilderness, and that burning bush caught his attention. God was communicating with Moses right from the beginning of this very visual lesson. What made that bush different from all the other bushes in the valley where Moses was walking? Only one thing: God was in the bush! God could have chosen any of the bushes in that valley to fill with His life and His power. He could have chosen any man, but He chose Moses. He did not choose Moses because of his great heritage, his excellent education, his eloquence, or his great potential. Moses was God's sovereign choice for this ministry, and he would become just like that bush. God would fill this weak man with His power and His glory, and God would display His greatness through him.

What a picture this is for you and me! There is nothing we can do that will result in the life of God poured out to people. God is not dependent on us. He could cause rocks to cry out and praise Him. He could use angels to fulfill His will. He does not need us, but He has chosen to use us. We find such value in the fact that we can be vessels for the very life of God, a means by which His eternal will is fulfilled.

God is the source of this new-covenant ministry, and He is the only means by which it is fulfilled. We bring nothing but responsive hearts, and God uses us to release His life, display His power, and fill the earth with His glory.

WALK ON THE LAND

Given the fleshly bent of our hearts, any talk of new-covenant ministry often results in a passive mind-set. "OK, if God is the initiative and I am called to be responsive, then I'm not going to do anything unless God specifically tells me to do this or that." But that's not what we see in Jesus' life. Rather, Jesus' ministry shows an element of aggressiveness in its responsiveness to the Father! Jesus said: "I always do the things that are pleasing to Him." We see that in God's call to Joshua also. Moses has died, and Joshua is the one God will use to lead His people to the Promised Land.

> After the death of Moses the servant of the LORD, the LORD said to Joshua the son of Nun, Moses' assistant, "Moses my servant is dead. Now therefore arise, go over this Jordan, you and all this people, into the land that I am giving to them, to the people of Israel. Every place that the sole of your foot will tread upon I have given to you, just as I promised to Moses." (Joshua 1:1-3)

After telling Joshua how vast the territory of Israel will be, God gives him the promise of His presence. Then the great challenge comes to Joshua: Be strong and courageous!

> From the wilderness and this Lebanon as far as the great river, the river Euphrates, all the land of the Hittites to the Great Sea toward the going down of the sun shall be your territory. No man shall be able to stand before you all the days of your life. Just as I was with Moses, so I will be with you. I will not leave you or forsake you. Be strong and courageous, for you shall cause this people to inherit the land that I swore to their fathers to give them. (Joshua 1:4-6)

God says to Joshua several times , "Be strong and coura-geous." But in the midst of this, He says, "I will give you every place where you set your foot." Now that is an interesting picture: God had already given the land to them, but they had to walk on it to possess it. What a description of new-covenant ministry! It is God who gives us ministry opportunities, and He fulfills them. He gives us the land, but we, too, need to walk on it to possess it.

God desires to open our eyes to ministry opportunities, to see what He is doing in our churches, to see places in which to serve, people to comfort or encourage, and others who are in need of counsel. He will cause us to be aware of our neighbors, our friends, our families who need Him. He will open our eyes to op-portunities and then He will move us by His Spirit to walk toward them. We walk aggressively in obedience, in the strength of the Lord, and we walk possessively on the land. God has already given us the ministry. We need to walk into it!

May God give us eyes to see what He is doing and hearts that aggressively obey Him as He leads us in triumph through Christ!

One of my early role models in missions was Hudson Taylor, who founded China Inland Mission. Already serving in that great nation in the nineteenth century, Taylor was called by God to go beyond the coastal areas where the gospel had been introduced and move into the interior of the country. The Holy Spirit showed him how to break down cultural barricrs by intimately identify-ing with the Chinese, seeming in almost every way to even be-come one of them. Hudson Taylor faced one obstacle after another as he sought to bring the love of Christ to Chinese peo-ple.

God has graciously allowed me to also serve His beautiful people in China, and our ministry has several teams of pastor trainers there, national leaders who are encouraging and equip-ping other nationals. The obstacles seemed overwhelming when we began, and they still seem that way today. But I learned a lesson from Hudson Taylor that has transformed my life and ministry—the work of God has three stages:

Impossible

Difficult

Done

We often dream that God will use us to do great things in ministry. Sometimes we feel that our dreams are too big. But our dreams, no matter how large, are always too small. When we learn that ministry is what God does and He is inviting us to walk with Him in the fulfillment of His purposes, he will teach us, too, that He is at work in us through His Holy Spirit, leading us into far more than we could ever dream!

> To him who is able to do far more abundantly than all that we ask or think, according to the power at work within us, to him be glory in the church and in Christ Jesus throughout all generations, forever and ever. Amen. (Ephesians 3:20-21)

QUESTIONS FOR COMMUNICATION AND APPLICATION

1. How would your life be different if you said only the things God told you to say and did only the things God told you to do, as Jesus did?

2. Are you able to enjoy the labor God has given you? Why or why not?

3. Where do you see evidences of old-covenant ministry in your life? Where do you see evidences of new-covenant ministry?

4. Where in your life do you tend to depend on yourself? Where do you see yourself still working to "make things happen" rather than trusting God to do His will?

5. In what areas do you need to be more aggressive in responding to ministry opportunities?

And the word of the LORD came to me, saying, "Jeremiah, what do you see?" And I said, "I see an almond branch." Then the LORD said to me, "You have seen well, for I am watching over my word to perform it."

Jeremiah 1:11-12

3
God's Creative Word

T hus far in our study, we have looked at how God begins ministry with vision—not so much a vision of what He will do with us but a vision of Himself. The fuller our vision of God, the more fruitful and effective our ministry will be. We have also discussed the fact that because ministry is what God does, He desires from us responsive hearts as we walk with Him in the fulfillment of His will.

As we continue in our study, we will look at the tool God uses in ministry: the creative power of His Word. When God called the prophets to Himself, He not only began their ministry with vision; He also commissioned them with the ministry of His Word. God never permitted the prophets to give their thoughts, their ideas, their impressions, or their solutions to His people. God limited them to what He told them to say. The words of men and women might be able to stimulate people's minds, but our words will never change another person's heart. Only God's words create life.

For us to more fully understand a commissioning with God's words, let's look at God's call of the young man Jeremiah to the ministry of a prophet. What vision did God give Jeremiah as He called him?

MY WORDS IN YOUR MOUTH

> The words of Jeremiah, the son of Hilkiah, one of the priests who were in Anathoth in the land of Benjamin, to whom the word of the LORD came in the days of Josiah the son of Amon, king of Judah, in the thirteenth year of his reign. It came also in the days of Jehoiakim the son of Josiah, king of Judah, and until the end of the eleventh year of Zedekiah, the son of Josiah, king of Judah, until the captivity of Jerusalem in the fifth month. (Jeremiah 1:1-3)

Jeremiah is often called the weeping prophet. This man had much to weep about. His ministry covered a period of forty years during which there was never any positive response on the part of God's people to the message God had entrusted to him. His heart was continually broken by the hard-hearted rebellion of God's people.

> The word of the LORD came to me, saying, "Before I formed you in the womb I knew you, and before you were born I consecrated you; I appointed you a prophet to the nations." (Jeremiah 1:4-5)

God wanted Jeremiah to know that the roots of his life and ministry went deeply into His heart. Before Jeremiah was formed in his mother's womb, he was known of God. Before he was born, he was set apart for this ministry and appointed by the Lord God as a prophet to the nations. Jeremiah would have great authority in his ministry! When we send ambassadors from our country to meet with the heads of foreign nations, they go with full authority, as if our president were standing there with them. They speak for our president. That is the kind of authority Jeremiah would have in his ministry. He was appointed by the Lord God.

That authority would bring the full weight of God's Word to his ministry.

How does Jeremiah respond to this call?

> Ah, Lord GOD! Behold, I do not know how to speak, for I am only a youth. (Jeremiah 1:6)

Just as we saw with Moses, Jeremiah was immediately caught up in the obstacles of his own weakness and inadequacy. "I'm too young, Lord. I do not know how to speak." If we are watching this scene take place in the heavenlies, do we see God holding His head in frustration and saying, "How could I have done it again? How could I have called another person who cannot speak well?" No! God is not frustrated with Jeremiah's response at all. Before God called this young man, He knew that Jeremiah did not have a thing to say that would make any difference in the lives of His people! God was putting no confidence in the words of this man. All of God's confidence was in His ability to speak through Jeremiah the words He desired and to fulfill all His will through this vessel He had chosen.

> But the LORD said to me, "Do not say, 'I am only a youth'; for to all to whom I send you, you shall go, and whatever I command you, you shall speak. Do not be afraid of them, for I am with you to deliver you, declares the LORD." Then the LORD put out his hand and touched my mouth. And the LORD said to me, "Behold, I have put my words in your mouth. See, I have set you this day over nations and over kingdoms, to pluck up and to break down, to destroy and to overthrow, to build and to plant." (Jeremiah 1:7-10)

Immediately we see God turning Jeremiah's focus from himself and his weakness to the resources of the living God! The repetition of God's assurance to Jeremiah of His authority, His presence, His strength, and His resource is so encouraging to us as well. "I'm sending you; I'm commanding you; I'm with you; I've put my words in your mouth; I'm appointing you," God tells this young man. Earlier, we talked about new-covenant ministry, ministry of which God is the source, ministry that is fulfilled by the power of the Lord God. We see that picture again in the passage above. God will surely be the source for Jeremiah's call, life, and ministry. As we continue in this passage, we see also God's command to Jeremiah to respond aggressively to His call.

> Dress yourself for work; arise, and say to them everything that I command you. Do not be dismayed by them, lest I dismay you before them. (Jeremiah 1:17)

We, too, need to understand that God is the source for our lives and ministries, that He will accomplish what He sets before us to do. Only in His strength is the work completed. There is also that aggressive response of wholehearted obedience with which we must come before the Lord. To stand up and walk in what God has called us to is a full picture of how God fulfills ministry. He is the only source; He is all the strength; He is all the means by which it is fulfilled. But we, like Jeremiah, and like the Lord Jesus, need to respond with hearts of aggressive obedience.

God sets before Jeremiah, and before you and me, another truth critical to effective ministry. To Jeremiah, so aware of his weakness and his inability to speak, God says, "Jeremiah, I have put my words in your mouth." Jeremiah's ministry will be a ministry of the words of the Lord God.

A MINISTRY OF OUR WORDS?

The Church in the developed world is a great enigma to us. Our theology generally is solid, and our knowledge is great, and we are so insightful. Do you realize that there has never been another time or place in history in which there has been a proliferation of the Scriptures such as we have today? While most Christian homes have several Bibles, even homes of many non-Christians contain Bibles. Churches seem to be on almost every corner, proclaiming the gospel week after week. The publication of Bibles and books about the Bible keep printing presses running day and night. Radio and television ministries fill the airwaves. We produce millions of audio and video CDs and offer seminars on every conceivable subject. There has never been in any time or in any place anything like we are experiencing with regard to Bible teaching. However, we must ask ourselves this question: Where are the corresponding holiness, power, and fruitfulness that we would expect to flow from this great proliferation of the Scriptures?

So much of what we have taking place today is a ministry of our own words. Even in many of our good churches, it is not uncommon for a minister to walk into the pulpit on Sunday morning and use a Bible verse as a "jumping off" point for twenty minutes of their own thoughts. That is an option God never permitted the prophets. God never gave them the freedom to speak their own words. God never permitted the disciples, the apostles, or His own Son to do that either. The sermons in the New Testament are filled with the Word of God. Jesus said to His disciples, "I do nothing on my own but speak just what the Father has taught me" (John 8:28).

Too many of us have taken options to ourselves that are deeply affecting the life of the church and the fruitfulness of ministry. We have too often placed our hope and confidence in our own words. We have become excited about what we have to say and are stimulated by our own ideas. God desires to call us back to a revival of the ministry of His Word. No matter now exciting, no matter how eloquent, no matter how beautifully presented or how persuasive are our words, nothing that we have to say will make any difference in anyone's life. Only God's words create life.

Of course, when we are talking about a ministry of God's words rather than our own, we do not mean just quoting the Scriptures. God has been pleased to use human instruments to preach His Word expressed through their own unique gifts and personality. We expound on the Scriptures, expose the truths there, and bring our own experiences and illustrations to bear on what we are teaching. We must be careful to say the same things God says and in the same way He says them!

Jeremiah raised a strong question that confronts us also:

> An appalling and horrible thing has happened in the land: the prophets prophesy falsely, and the priests rule at their direction; my people love to have it so, but what will you do when the end comes? (Jeremiah 5:30-31)

Any time we stand in our own authority, we are in a very dangerous place. When we speak forth our own thoughts and give our own ideas, impressions, and solutions, we are walking in activity that is no ministry at all; we are creating a desert and inviting God's judgment. As in Jeremiah's time, our people love it so, but what will we do at the end of it? We are greatly in need of a revival of the ministry of God's Word.

"WE DID IT FOR HIM"

Earlier, we saw how God called Ezekiel with a vision of His glory. Look with me further into God's preparation of that young man for the ministry of His Word.

> He said to me, "Son of man, stand on your feet, and I will speak with you." And as he spoke to me, the Spirit entered into me and set me on my feet, and I heard him speaking to me. And he said to me, "Son of man, I send you to the people of Israel, to nations

of rebels, who have rebelled against me. They and their fathers have transgressed against me to this very day." (Ezekiel 2:1-3)

God permitted no delusions of grandeur for Ezekiel at the beginning of his work. The people to whom Ezekiel is called as a prophet are a nation in rebellion against the Lord. But God would seal in Ezekiel a heart of faithfulness:

> The descendants also are impudent and stubborn: I send you to them, and you shall say to them, "Thus says the Lord GOD." And whether they hear or refuse to hear (for they are a rebellious house) they will know that a prophet has been among them. And you, son of man, be not afraid of them, nor be afraid of their words, though briers and thorns are with you and you sit on scorpions. Be not afraid of their words, nor be dismayed at their looks, for they are a rebellious house. And you shall speak my words to them, whether they hear or refuse to hear, for they are a rebellious house. (Ezekiel 2:4-7)

Twice in the space of just a few verses, God says to Ezekiel: "You speak my Word to them whether they listen or not." We must understand this truth about how God sees effective ministry. We tend to be pragmatists, continually measuring the effects, while God is measuring the message and the messenger. In our culture, whatever "works" becomes "right." Before long, the result of that pragmatism is a message that can be marketed, and we begin to give people what they are willing to buy. Effective ministry in the eyes of God is never measured by the response of the people. It is always, only, measured by the faithfulness of the messengers to the message that has been committed to them.

A few years ago I had the privilege of teaching a conference on the "ministry of God's Word" at a Wycliffe Bible Translators center in South America. We had a wonderful time of fellowship and ministry around the Word of God. The people were so encouraging in their responses that I was almost embarrassed at the gra-

Adequate!

cious and wonderful things they said to me about the way in which the Scriptures touched their hearts. I did not understand the significance of their responses until the last evening of my visit as I was having dinner in the home of the director. His wife said to me, "When we came to South America about twenty years ago, we were assigned an Indian tribe and began translating the Scriptures into their language." You might know something of the process that is involved in this. A linguist would go to a tribal group that does not have a written language and, after learning the spoken language, would begin to reduce it to a written language. The translator would then teach the people to read their own language. When the translation of the Scriptures is completed, the tribal people have the Word of God in their heart language. This process usually takes about twenty years.

As this gracious servant of the Lord continued, she said, "We worked at the Indian village and spent as much time with them as we could. We were teaching the Scriptures to them while we were translating. When we came toward the end of the project, the people were becoming more and more involved in the drug production and less and less interested in the Scriptures. When we finished the translation of the New Testament in their language and scheduled the dedication service, no one even came! I was so angry and bitter. We gave our lives so that they could have the Word of God in their language. When we concluded what was almost a life's work, they didn't even want it! I have not been able to handle this bitter disappointment in my heart." Then she said, "God has been speaking to me in these days and it almost seems as if He has been washing His Word over my soul. He is opening my eyes to understand some new things. I'm just beginning to realize now that we did it for Him. That is the only thing that makes any sense in all this. We did it for God."

That is the only thing that makes any difference in ministry. We do it for Him. We have almost completely lost a vision for the great, eternal value of proclaiming the Person of God and the words that He speaks just because He has called us to do it. We must do it for Him.

THE WORD ASSIMILATED

"Son of man, listen to what I say to you. Do not rebel like that rebellious house; open your mouth and eat what I give you." Then I looked, and I saw a hand stretched out to me. In it was a scroll, which he unrolled before me. On both sides of it were written words of lament and mourning and woe. (Ezekiel 2:8-10)

We find here one of the most vivid pictures in all the Scriptures and one of our most important lessons in preparation for ministry. God hands Ezekiel a scroll and tells him to eat it. On the scroll were written hard words of mourning, lamentation, and woe.

He said to me, "Son of man, eat whatever you find here. Eat this scroll, and go, speak to the house of Israel." So I opened my mouth, and he gave me this scroll to eat. And he said to me, "Son of man, feed your belly with this scroll that I give you and fill your stomach with it." Then I ate it, and it was in my mouth as sweet as honey. And he said to me, "Son of man, go to the house of Israel and speak with my words to them." (Ezekiel 3:1-4)

We have here a strong visual description of God's preparation for ministry—first a vision of His glory and then a call to faithfulness. Even more amazingly, we see God hand Ezekiel the scroll on which His word is written. "Eat the scroll, Ezekiel; fill your body with this scroll." The words are bitter, but Ezekiel says, "When I ate it, it was sweet as honey to my mouth." You might remember that Jeremiah had a similar experience. He said, "Your

93

words were found, and I ate them, and your word became to me a joy and the delight of my heart." (Jeremiah 15:16)

I do not know what your day has been like. It could be that you awoke early and had a good breakfast. Maybe someone who loves you even fixed a breakfast of bacon, eggs, or pancakes; perhaps you had a bowl of cereal. Maybe you got up late and grabbed a piece of toast and a cup of coffee on the way out the door. For lunch you could have had a bowl of soup or a sandwich. But something amazing, even miraculous, took place in the hours after you ate. Food that you ate this morning and at noon is no longer cereal and toast or bacon and eggs. Through the amazing process of assimilation, it began to become part of you; it began to be incorporated into every cell of your body.

God is setting a powerful picture before Ezekiel. He must know that before he can minister God's Word with authority and power, in a way that brings the life of God to the people of God, that Word must first become a living part of who he is. It must be assimilated into his person; it must be incorporated into the fabric of his heart and life. The assimilation of God's Word is God's preparation for the ministry of His Word.

INCARNATION AND LIFE

If we are teaching a Sunday school class, leading a Bible study, or preaching a sermon, how do we prepare when we have opportunities to share our faith with others or to counsel and encourage them? Can we take a Sunday school quarterly, add some stories to the outline, and bring it to people, hoping that God will use it to release His life to them? Is good communication like "plugging a CD into the back of our heads" and speaking the words that we heard someone famous say in hopes that ministry will happen? No! God told Ezekiel that before he could bring His

Word to His people, that Word must first come alive within him; so it is with you and me. We cannot bypass the process of the Word of God coming alive within us and being incorporated into the fabric of our hearts and lives, as a means of God giving His life to His people through us.

There is another word that we use to describe this process. When we talk about food, the word is assimilation. When we talk about the Word of God, the term is incarnation—the Word becoming flesh. Before God can minister His Word through us in a life-giving way, that Word must first become flesh within us. It must be incarnated into the whole of our beings.

Perhaps the greatest preacher that ever walked the land of America was George Whitefield, an unbeliever in his early years but part of a "holy club" that was very disciplined in its pursuits. The members of this club tried to live holy and disciplined lives by their own strength. In the extreme discipline and rigorous schedule, Whitefield's health was broken, and he almost lost his life. Then God gloriously saved him. It took years for him to recover his strength. During that time he said, "I would take the Scriptures and Matthew Henry's commentary, and I would pore over every line and word until it became a part of my own living soul." Later in his ministry, he often preached forty hours a week! It was from the overflow of what God built into his heart during those years as he was studying the Word of God that he was able to minister in that way.

Just as with Ezekiel and George Whitefield, before we can minister the Word of God in a way that gives His life to His people, that Word first must become a living part of who we are. It must be incorporated into the fabric of our hearts and lives. I want to look further with you into this process through which God's Word comes alive in us in preparation for ministry.

IF YOU HAVE EARS TO HEAR...

In Mark 4, we find a sermon that the Lord Jesus preached to the multitudes and then again to His disciples. This was one of those times when Jesus was preaching and there were so many people by the seaside that there was no room for Him to stand in front of them and speak. Thus, He got into a boat and began to speak from it. I can visualize the scene and hear Him saying, "Peter, would you row me out a little way." After Peter rowed Him out, He began to preach.

> "Listen! A sower went out to sow. And as he sowed, some seed fell along the path, and the birds came and devoured it. Other seed fell on rocky ground, where it did not have much soil, and immediately it sprang up, since it had no depth of soil. And when the sun rose it was scorched, and since it had no root, it withered away. Other seed fell among thorns, and the thorns grew up and choked it, and it yielded no grain. And other seeds fell into good soil and produced grain, growing up and increasing and yielding thirtyfold and sixtyfold and a hundredfold." And he said, "He who has ears to hear, let him hear." (Mark 4:3-9)

"Thus endeth the sermon for today. OK, Peter, you can row me back in." The message could not have taken ten minutes! We can see the disciples looking at one another and saying, "What in the world is He talking about?" So later, Jesus preached an explanatory sermon to His disciples.

> When he was alone, those around him with the twelve asked him about the parables. And he said to them, "To you has been given the secret of the kingdom of God, but for those outside everything is in parables, so that they may indeed see but not perceive, and may indeed hear but not understand, lest they should turn and be forgiven." (Mark 4:10-12)

Jesus taught in parables for two reasons. One was a sifting process. He was looking for those who were drawn by the Holy Spirit, who would come to Him after the teaching and say, "What is the meaning of this? Tell me more." He was looking for those whose hearts were hungry. The parables were also a process of judging His people. The truth was purposely hidden because of the hardhearted rebellion of the religious leaders.

[Jesus] said to them, "Do you not understand this parable? How then will you understand all the parables?" (Mark 4:13)

There seems to be something so basic about the parable of the sower and the soils in Jesus' ministry to His disciples. We need to see the truths He brought to them here.

HEARTS THAT ARE HARDENED

The sower sows the word. (Mark 4:14)

The seed we are talking about is the very Word of God!

These are the ones along the path, where the word is sown: when they hear, Satan immediately comes and takes away the word that is sown in them. (Mark 4:15)

We can visualize what Jesus is describing. We can see the farmer begin to sow after he has prepared the field. Sometimes a farmer's field would be bordered by a road. As people walked down that road on their way back and forth to town, there might be a flock of sheep or goats in the road, or perhaps an oxcart, and the people would walk around it on the edges of the field. After a time, the ground between the road and the field would become hardened. When the farmer sowed the seed, some of the seed would fall onto that hard, packed ground, and before the seed could take root, the birds would come and eat it.

Jesus is teaching us that some people have hearts like that hard-packed soil. Some people's hearts have become so hardened that when God speaks His Word, Satan is there to steal it away before it can take root. The hardness of their hearts resists the penetration of the Word of God.

Sometimes, when we see people going through very difficult and painful experiences in their lives, we see them turning to themselves rather than to God for His mercy and compassion. Every time they turn away from God and toward themselves, their hearts become a little harder. The same sun that melts wax hardens clay. People can go through the same experiences and respond in two completely different ways. Some are drawn to God in their pain, and His mercy keeps softening their hearts. Others keep turning inward, and their hearts are hardened over and over in the process. When God speaks His word, their hearts are so hard they cannot receive it. Satan steals it away before they can respond.

HEARTS THAT ARE SHALLOW

These are the ones sown on rocky ground: the ones who, when they hear the word, immediately receive it with joy. And they have no root in themselves, but endure for a while; then, when tribulation or persecution arises on account of the word, immediately they fall away. (Mark 4:16-17)

Immediately they receive it with joy, and immediately they fall away! Now as Jesus talks about rocky soil, He is not describing soil that is filled with rocks. He is picturing a thin layer of soil over a layer of rock. When the farmer sows the seed, because there is a layer of soil there, the seed begins to grow. However, because there is no depth to the soil, the root can go down only so far before it hits the rock. When the sprout comes up and the sun becomes full in its heat, life cannot be sustained since there is no depth to the root system, and the plant shrivels up and dies. Jesus said that some people have hearts like that, hearts that are shallow and cannot support life to the point of fruitfulness.

I have always enjoyed gardening. A few years ago we had the privilege of building a house in the Chicago suburbs. The lot we purchased was large enough for a good-sized garden. Before we built the house, I planned on planting my garden in a certain area on the lot. Unfortunately, I did not communicate well with the fellow who was putting in the septic field. Because he had a lot more rocks than he needed, he dumped a big portion of them in part of the area where I wanted to plant my garden. When the final grading of the lot was done after the house was completed, the workers smoothed the rock over and put more dirt over it all. It looked good. In the spring, I planted my garden, and in a few weeks, everything was coming up beautifully. Then in one area all the plants shriveled up and died. I did not realize what was happening until the hard summer rains began to expose the rocks. The soil was too shallow to support life. Jesus says that some people have hearts like that. The soil of their hearts is too shallow to support life that will result in fruitfulness.

How often do we have people coming into our churches who are so excited about the teaching, the worship, or the warmth of the fellowship? It is such an encouragement to have folks like that come and cheer the rest of us on. Sometimes, however, after a few months or a few years, they are gone as quickly as they came. Some problem or difficulty arose that they could not deal with. We look around and say, "Whatever happened to so and so?" They flared out just as quickly as they flared up!

Often, people who come only because they are excited about the preaching, the music, or the relationships are not prepared for what the "real Christian life" is all about. Sometimes, as Jesus said, when afflictions, trouble, and persecution come because of the Word, they fall away. When they are confronted with the pain, loss, and pressure that are all a part of the normal Christian experience, they say, "Hey, this isn't what I expected. This isn't what I'm interested in." And they are gone.

Suppose we went tonight to a shopping mall and asked the people who pass by, "How do you see God? What is your view of Him?" Because most people believe in God, many would say, "I know that God is there and if I ever get into trouble, He is there to help me." The image many people in this world have is that God is there waiting for their call to rescue them in a time of need. They see a God who lives to meet their expectations. Of course, many in our churches also have this view of God. Some of our churches today talk of a God who lives to make us healthy, wealthy, and happy. Real life does not often fit into that picture. When sickness, affliction, persecution, painful relationships, and financial pressures come, we cannot handle it. Jesus tells His disciples that some people need the soil of their hearts deepened; their hearts are just too shallow. When we demand that God function according to our own images of Him and our own expectations, the soil is not deep enough to support life. When the hot sun of persecution and afflictions comes out, the plant will shrivel up and die.

HEARTS THAT ARE FILLED WITH WEEDS

Others are the ones sown among thorns. They are those who hear the word, but the cares of the world and the deceitfulness of riches and the desires for other things enter in and choke the word, and it proves unfruitful. (Mark 4:18-19)

Again, as the farmer sows the seeds, they begin to grow. But the seeds are not the only thing growing in the soil; it is also filled with thorns and thistles. Before the seeds can produce fruit, the thorns and thistles choke them out, and they die. Every time I read this passage, my own heart is convicted about how I handle the thorns and thistles in my life. Sometimes rather than weed them out in the painful process of obedience, I find myself cultivating them, feeding and watering them because of the temptation to love those things that steal away my life with God.

Jesus describes these thorns and thistles as the worries of this life, the deceitfulness of wealth, and the desire for other things. Many of us are distracted and stifled by the things of this world. We get distracted by the possibilities of wealth and fall prey to the materialism that is consuming our world. Satan has convinced even many of God's people that their lives can be filled up by things.

Some Bible versions translate "the cares of the world" as "the worries of this life." This life has a myriad of worries that would drain hope from our hearts. There are worries that are specific to each period of history. Brokenness in families, financial pressures, and fears about the future are worries of this age. In another sense, there are unique worries to the season in which we are living personally. There are things that our enemy will bring to us at each time of life to steal away our responsiveness to the Word of God.

When we are teenagers and God calls us to live for Christ, we might respond by saying, "Lord, I really want to do that; I'm headed in that direction, but right now my friends are so important to me. I am never going to have a time like this again when I can be free to enjoy my friends and develop these relationships. Later on, I'm going to live completely for Christ."

When we get into university, God will call us to a walk of discipleship, developing a hunger for Himself and the words He speaks. We might say, "God, I'm interested in that, and I want that for my life, but right now I have to give myself to my studies. These courses are so consuming, and if I don't get this right, I'm not going to be able to be used by you later on. I just have to pour myself into my education. After my education is over, then I'll be able to pursue you and your Word."

After the university, there is a career to develop. God calls us to orient all our resources around Him and His Kingdom, and we say, "God, I want to do that, too, but right now I have to put all my time into the development of my career. It's going to take so many extra hours to build a foundation for the rest of my working life. But, God, I know that if I do this right, if I put in the time now, later on, after I have built this business, I can actually do this job in only half the time it takes now. I will be able to give a lot of time to the church. I might even be able to retire early and go to the mission field."

Then comes marriage. God calls us to a love for Christ that consumes our hearts. We say, "God, we want that, too, but right now we want to grow together, to know one another and to enjoy each other. In a few years the children will be here, and there will never be another time like this. It is so enjoyable to sleep late on Sunday mornings after our demanding work responsibilities all week and just enjoy each other. With the work responsibilities and all the other pressures, Sunday morning is the only time we have for that. Later on in our lives we'll be able to pursue Christ with all our hearts."

Then, of course, we must prepare for education for our children. And then we need to plan for our retirement, and we want to enjoy it, so we say, "I've put in my time in the church. Now it is time for some of the younger people."

Do you realize that tomorrow never comes? Are you aware that tomorrow is a lie? Tomorrow is one of Satan's most powerful weapons against the lives of God's people. There is no such thing as tomorrow. Today is the only day God has given to us to walk with Him and to work with Him in the building of His church. If we will not walk with Him today, we will not walk with Him tomorrow, because tomorrow is only an illusion. It never comes.

As it is said, "Today, if you hear his voice, do not harden your hearts as in the rebellion." (Hebrews 3:15)

Today is the only day God has given to us to serve Him. If not now, when? How many, even of God's people, have seen their lives stolen away in a thousand "tomorrows" that have never come.

HEAR THE WORD AND ACCEPT IT

Those that were sown on the good soil are the ones who hear the word and accept it and bear fruit, thirtyfold and sixtyfold and a hundredfold. (Mark 4:20)

What is the difference between the first three kinds of soil and the good soil that produces fruit? Only one thing: It hears the Word and accepts it. There is a receptivity in the soil and a responsiveness to the seed that is sown, and God's Word grows to fruitfulness—thirty, sixty or even a hundredfold.

Later in the chapter, Mark records another parable about a farmer.

"The kingdom of God is as if a man should scatter seed on the ground. He sleeps and rises night and day, and the seed sprouts and grows; he knows not how. The earth produces by itself, first the blade, then the ear, then the full grain in the ear. But when the grain is ripe, at once he puts in the sickle, because the harvest has come." And he said, "With what can we compare the kingdom of God, or what parable shall we use for it?" (Mark 4:26-30)

What a picture! The farmer can prepare the field and sow the seed, but then what can he do? Is there anything he can do to make the seed grow? No. After his work is completed, he goes to bed. Even while he is sleeping, the seed begins to sprout. He does not even know how it happens. All of the life is in the seed. When the time for harvest comes, he puts in the sickle. Is there anything we can do to cause the Word of God to grow within us? No. All of the life is in the Word. The farmer who sows the seed in the soil that he has prepared cannot cause it to grow. We cannot cause the Word of God to grow within us either, but we can prepare the soil, the environment of our hearts. The life is in the seed.

Jesus sets before us some valuable teaching that ties these two parables together:

> He said to them, "Is a lamp brought in to be put under a basket, or under a bed, and not on a stand? For nothing is hidden except to be made manifest; nor is anything secret except to come to light. If anyone has ears to hear, let him hear." And he said to them, "Pay attention to what you hear: with the measure you use, it will be measured to you, and still more will be added to you. For to the one who has, more will be given, and from the one who has not, even what he has will be taken away." (Mark 4:21-25)

THE STEWARDSHIP OF OUR HEARTS

As Jesus teaches about light revealed and knowledge given, He is talking about stewardship. We are stewards of the truth that God opens to us and the life that He reveals. This is the teaching that ties the two parables together; the teaching about the parable of the sower and soils and the story of the farmer are both about stewardship. We are stewards of the heart that God has given to us.

I am so glad that Jesus is talking about hearts rather than lives, because hearts can change. Every one of us can look back over our lives and remember times when our hearts were characterized by each of those kinds of soils. There were times when our hearts were hardened; we were not able to hear the Word of God; we were not able to receive it. The seed of the Word could not penetrate. There were times when our hearts were shallow and we demanded that God function according to our images and expectations; when real life problems and afflictions came along, we wanted to quit.

There were times when our hearts were characterized by the thorns and thistles. As God's Spirit desired His Word to grow, it was continually choked out by our desires for other things. The worries of this life kept stealing away our responsiveness to God. And then by God's grace there were times when God spoke His Word and it began to grow and produce a crop—thirty, sixty and a hundredfold. Hearts can change. Our hope is in a God who changes hearts. He does it as we faithfully bring His Word and respond to it.

What is the difference between the good soil and the other kinds of soil? Only one thing: The hearers respond to the Word and accept it. There is a pattern of responsiveness in the soil to the Word of God. There is nothing that we can do to cause the Word of God to grow within us; all the life is in the seed. However, we can participate with God in the preparation of the soil of our hearts. We can till the soil so that it is soft and deep and free. We can participate with God in the preparation of the soil of our hearts so that we can hear when God speaks to us and accept what He tells us. We hear and respond, and the Word grows to fruitfulness.

Two times in this teaching Jesus says, "He who has ears to hear let him hear." Not everyone has ears to hear. The ability to hear God is a gift of the Holy Spirit. If He has given us ears to hear, we are stewards of the truth He gives and of the light He reveals to us. He calls us to respond in obedience. We hear the Word and accept it, and His Word overflows through us in lives of fruitfulness to His glory.

HIS COMMANDMENT IS ETERNAL LIFE

If we were to choose two verses that summarize how Jesus saw His life and His ministry, I think they might very well be John 12:49-50. Jesus is speaking to His disciples just before the "upper room discourse," those last hours He spent with them before He went to the cross.

> I have not spoken on my own authority, but the Father who sent me has himself given me a commandment—what to say and what to speak. And I know that his commandment is eternal life. What I say, therefore, I say as the Father has told me. (John 12:49-50)

We see the same repetition in John's Gospel that we discussed earlier. Jesus pictures His Father as the initiative in His life and ministry; Jesus walks responsively before Him. Jesus did not speak of His own accord; everything began with His Father. The Father who sent Him commanded Him what to say and how to say it. Then Jesus says, "I know that His command is eternal life." That is why Jesus walked and ministered the way He did.

He saw a clear relationship between the words God spoke, His life being poured out to His people, and His obedience as central to that process. "I know that His command is eternal life." Do you see a relationship between the words God speaks and life springing forth within you and through you as you respond in obedience?

When we walk out of our church buildings on Sunday mornings after the worship and the message, one of the most common things said to the pastor is, "You really gave me something to think about today." This is a very revealing statement, because many of us really do believe that God gives us His Word for us to think about it. In reality, God has very little interest in stimulating our thoughts and expanding our minds with new insights. It is His desire to transform our hearts and to build His own heart into us. He would give us His values, His motives, His priorities, His passions, and His pursuits. This process grows within us as we respond to the Word of God with hearts of obedience, rather than seeing a sermon as intellectual stimulation. We, too, need to see the relationship between the words God speaks, our obedience, and the life of God being poured out.

I would like for us to place two well-known Scripture verses alongside each another in our minds and hearts. Paul said in Philippians 2,

> Being found in human form, he humbled himself by becoming obedient to the point of death, even death on a cross. (Philippians 2:8)

Link that with another well-known passage in John 1:

> The Word became flesh and dwelt among us, and we have seen his glory, glory as of the only Son from the Father, full of grace and truth. (John 1:14)

Jesus became obedient to the point of death, and the Word became flesh and dwelt among us. John is describing the incarnation. The "contact point" in the process of the incarnation was the obediencc in thc heart of the Son of God! He became obedient to His Father, even to the point of death on a cross, and the Word became flesh and dwelt among us. God poured out His life to us in the obedience of His Son.

I would remind you of the "big picture" with which we began. We discussed a commitment to the ministry of the Word of God, and God's process of preparing Ezekiel for that work. Before Ezekiel could minister the Word of God with power and authority in a way that released the life of God to the people of God, that

Adequate!

Word first had to become a living part of his person. It had to be assimilated, incorporated, and incarnated into his life.

The same is true for you and me. When we are teaching, preaching, counseling, or encouraging, God's Word must first become a living part of who we are before we can minister that Word in a way that would bring His life to His people. Is it only the gaining of insight and interesting information that we can pass on to people hoping for transformation? No, there is a process that cannot be bypassed. The Word comes alive within us in the process of obedience. It is when God speaks His Word to us and we respond with whole hearts of obedience that the seed begins to grow to fruitfulness. That is hearing the Word and accepting it!

What does this look like for you and me? When God talks to us about our finances, we say, "Yes Lord," and we respond with whole hearts of obedience. When He talks to us about our sexual desires, we say, "Yes Lord," and we respond with whole hearts of obedience. When He talks to us about our marriage relationships and our ministries to our children, our time priorities, our attitude toward our jobs, and about personal holiness, we keep saying, "Yes Lord, Yes Lord, Yes Lord." We hear the Word and we accept it. The Word of God comes to life within us, begins to grow to fruitfulness, and overflows through us into a ministry of fruitfulness to the very glory of God.

GOD PERFORMS HIS WORD

Let us return now to God's call to Jeremiah. God sets before him, and before you and me, another truth that will transform our ministries.

> The word of the LORD came to me, saying, "Jeremiah, what do you see?" And I said, "I see an almond branch." Then the LORD

108

said to me, "You have seen well, for I am watching over my word to perform it." (Jeremiah 1:11-12)

We find here a "play on words." The almond tree was called "the watcher" in the land of Israel because it was the first tree to bloom in the spring. The people of Israel would watch for the almond tree to bloom and when it did, they would know that spring was returning after the deadness and dryness of winter. Here in the Chicago area we look for the first robin to come back in the springtime. We see the robins returning from the South, and we know that spring is "just around the corner." The Israelites would watch for the almond tree to bloom. "What do you see, Jeremiah?" says God. "I see the branch of an almond tree," responds Jeremiah. "You have seen correctly. I am watching to see that my Word is fulfilled."

What would keep Jeremiah from losing heart in those forty years of ministry with no positive response on the part of God's people to the Word and the message God had entrusted to him? Two things: first God's call to faithfulness, and then the confidence that God fulfills His Word. Jeremiah would know from the very beginning of his ministry that God performs the words He speaks!

Where is our confidence in ministry? Is there anything we can say that will change anyone's life or any eloquence of ours that can produce holiness in the hearts of God's people? Are there any encouraging words that can give them hope or anything that will bring healing to their pain? Is there anything to call them to obedience? No! Only the words of God can fulfill these things. All of our hope in ministry is in a God who brings to pass the words He speaks.

There is a great passage in Isaiah's prophecy that reveals this same powerful truth to us.

> As the rain and the snow come down from heaven and do not re-
> turn there but water the earth, making it bring forth and sprout,
> giving seed to the sower and bread to the eater, so shall my word
> be that goes out from my mouth; it shall not return to me empty,
> but it shall accomplish that which I purpose, and shall succeed
> in the thing for which I sent it. (Isaiah 55:10-11)

As God draws that picture in our minds of the process of pre-
cipitation and evaporation, we have an understanding of the creative power of the words He speaks. The rain and snow come
down from the heavens and eventually they return to the heavens. Before they return, however, they cause the earth to become
fruitful and productive, furnishing seed to the sower and bread
to the eater. God tells us that this is exactly what His Word does
in the lives of people! His Word goes forth from Him; His Word returns to Him. Before His Word returns, however, just like the rain
and the snow do with the earth, His Word causes the lives of people to become fruitful and productive. God is speaking of the creative power of His Word! Just as God spoke in the beginning of
time and the worlds came into existence, so He speaks His Word
in our hearts, causing new things to come alive day by day. This
is our hope in ministry. We have a God who is able to create life
where there is no life by means of His Word and His Spirit. He fulfills His Word. Our confidence must be placed in the eternal,
powerfully creative Word of God.

WOULD YOU GIVE ME A HEART LIKE THAT?

The first time I went to South America, I had the privilege of
teaching a series of conferences to missionaries, pastors and lay
leaders. One of these conferences was in a jungle village by the
name of Linares. I went with my friend Américo Saavedra, who is
on the staff of HCJB Global in Quito, Ecuador. He has also
worked with us at Leadership Resources for many years. We

drove four hours from Quito down the Andes Mountains and came to a town called Chaco. There we were going to meet the pastor of the church and go on to the village of Linares.

Arriving at Chaco in the midst of a blinding rainstorm, we waited and we waited, but the rain did not let up. Finally the pastor said, "If we're going to make it to the village in time for the evening meeting, we need to leave." Américo had not told me that the remainder of the trip would be made by mule. The rain continued to pour down as we packed our bags on the mules and rode out of town. I was second in line, behind the pastor's young son. About two blocks out of town, the pastor's son turned his mule down a mountain path so steep that he disappeared from my sight immediately. Of course, my mule just followed along. I have a tremendous fear of heights, and I could visualize my mule losing its footing on that steep mountain trail in the slippery mud and tumbling down the mountain. I was trying to stop my mule and get off, and the pastor was running up beside me (he could not speak English and I could not speak Spanish) waving frantically, trying to get me to stay on that mule. I have never been as frightened in my life!

As it wound down the mountain, the trail was narrower than the mule. When we got down to the bottom, there was the raging river with a suspension bridge over it (I'm sure you have seen them in missionary presentations). As we were getting onto the bridge, Américo said, "We lost a mule off this bridge last month." He was enjoying every minute of this whole experience as he watched the expression of fear on my face. After another two hours we made it up another steep mountain and down the other side. Although I still do not know how I ever lived through it, God was gracious.

We finally arrived at the village where forty pastors and church leaders had come for those days of ministry. Many of them had walked for two days to hear the Word of God, which greatly humbled my heart. We had a tremendous time in the Scriptures. Américo spoke that first evening, and then the next morning I taught on the heart of a servant, as Américo translated for me. I finished what I believe God had given to me to say and whispered to Américo, "Why don't you close in prayer?" He had hardly said, "Amen," when someone from the congregation began to pray. Then another and another. Of course, I could not understand what they were saying, but Américo leaned over to me and said, "God is at work here." On and on they prayed. Finally, Américo said, "I think we might as well go sit down." They prayed longer than we had taught. Again he leaned over to me and said, "They are asking God to create within them the heart of a servant, to give them a love for one another that is visible to their enemies around them. There are people in those villages who are persecuting them. They are praying that their enemies would see that they come from Christ by the way they love one another, and as they become servants of each other." I sat in that little jungle village in Ecuador, crying out to God, and saying, "God, would you give me a heart like that? Would you give me a heart that responds so wholly and quickly to the words You speak? Would You give me a heart like that?"

BROKEN CISTERNS

In Jeremiah 2, God summarizes for His prophet the condition of His people's hearts:

> My people have committed two evils: they have forsaken me, the fountain of living waters, and hewed out cisterns for themselves, broken cisterns that can hold no water. (Jeremiah 2:13)

Sometimes when God's people would be in the midst of a battle with their enemies, or when they were under a siege, their enemies would cut them off from their water supplies. The children of Israel would then go up to the mountains where the streams flowed in the springtime as the rains came. They would build a cistern in the place of that stream so that as the stream would flow, it would fill the cistern and they would have a supply of water. However, often their workmanship was poor and the cisterns would break. Then as the rains came in the springtime, and the streams began to flow with such power, they would pick up many things along the way. The river would pick up broken tree limbs, dead animals, dirt and rocks, all of which would flow into the cistern. Because the cistern was broken, the water would flow out; all they were left with were the dead and broken things of the world.

God's people had forsaken Him, the very source of living water, to make for themselves cisterns—broken cisterns that could hold no water. What a picture that is of life without God and of religious activity apart from the words God speaks!

So when we sit before a pastoral search committee or a mission board and they ask us: "What is your vision for this church? What is your vision for this position?" we can be free to respond: "I am going to pursue a growing vision of God and ask Him to show me by His Spirit how to walk with Him in what He is doing. With all my heart and strength, I will seek to respond aggressively to God's leading, wholeheartedly obey His word and lead this church, or this mission, into the work God has prepared for us as He fills the earth with His glory."

QUESTIONS FOR COMMUNICATION AND APPLICATION

1. Do you often see yourself placing confidence in your own words, ideas, or insights as you seek to minister to people? How

would "speaking God's Word" affect the way you respond to ministry situations?

2. How would your ministry change if you placed the emphasis on your faithfulness to what God had entrusted to you rather than on the responses of people?

3. In the parable of the sower and the soils, which soil most closely resembles your own heart? Why?

4. As you look at the process of obedience and the Word of God coming alive within you, what areas of your life does God bring to your mind in which you need to "hear the Word and accept it?"

But we have this treasure in jars of clay, to show that the surpassing power belongs to God and not to us.

2 Corinthians 4:7

4

The Treasure and the Vessel

G od is eternally committed to developing us as vessels for the ministry of His life. God tells us that we were chosen in Christ before the foundation of the world. For years before we were born, God was choosing our ancestors so that we would be just the person He was calling us to be. God wove us in our mother's womb, and in all our days, in the sovereignty of God's timing, He has allowed circumstances, situations and relationships to develop, continually molding us into the image of His Son. Each one of us is uniquely His workmanship, and God is shaping us as vessels for ministry and for His glory.

A PROGRESSIVE WALK OF OBEDIENCE

In 2 Peter 1, Peter gives us an understanding of the progressive process in which we walk toward all that God has called us to be in His Son. In fact, He sets before us a series of concentric circles, developing again and again a picture of how our lives flow out of who God is:

Adequate!

> Simeon Peter, a servant and apostle of Jesus Christ, to those who have obtained a faith of equal standing with ours by the righteousness of our God and Savior Jesus Christ. (2 Peter 1:1)

The faith we have received is the result of the righteousness of God:

> May grace and peace be multiplied to you in the knowledge of God and of Jesus our Lord. (2 Peter 1:2)

Grace and peace, those gifts from God for which we hunger, are multiplied in our lives over and over again as our knowledge of Him grows:

> His divine power has granted to us all things that pertain to life and godliness, through the knowledge of him who called us to his own glory and excellence. (2 Peter 1:3)

Sometimes we fall into the trap of saying, "If I just had more faith, if only I had more strength, if God would give me more patience, if God would just do this or that in my life, I could be more mature and God could use me." Often we wait for God to do more in our lives so that we can be what He has called us to be. However, He has already granted to us everything we need for life and godliness! We lack nothing as the people of God. He has granted all of this to us through His divine power and through the knowledge of Him who called us by His own glory and goodness.

Isn't this a beautiful description of the basis for God's call in our lives? Did we bring any performance worthy of His notice or any potential to show why He should consider using us? No, there is only one reason for God's call to you and me: the glory and excellence of His person:

> He has granted to us his precious and very great promises, so that through them you may become partakers of the divine na-

ture, having escaped from the corruption that is in the world because of sinful desire. For this very reason, make every effort to supplement your faith with virtue. (2 Peter 1:4-5a)

We need to see the priorities of our Father here. His call to us is not primarily to service. He will use us by His grace to His glory in the work He entrusts to us, but His first call is to share His nature. God will build His heart into us by His Spirit. Who we are in Him is always more important than what we are doing for Him.

Peter is setting before us an aggressive, progressive walk of obedience in the environment of our faith. He tells us that adding goodness to our faith is moral excellence. This is a singly focused commitment of spirit, soul and body, to the call God has set before us in His Son.

And virtue with knowledge. (2 Peter 1:5b)

Peter is moving us to a deeper understanding of the Person of God and His purposes in sending His Son. However, when God talks about knowledge, He is not referring to information; He is talking about relationships. This knowledge is not based on information or facts gained about another person. "Knowing" is a relationship of life, intimately and deeply shared.

And knowledge with self-control. (2 Peter 1:6a)

Self-control is learning to live with our bodies as our servants, rather than living the way this world teaches us to live, as slaves of our bodies.

And self-control with steadfastness. (2 Peter 1:6b)

Continuing to walk in the face of great trials, tribulations, temptations, and afflictions, we do not give up when the Christian life no longer measures up to our hopes and expectations. God builds into us a spirit of endurance as we walk with Him.

And steadfastness with godliness. (2 Peter 1:6c)

A character and lifestyle consistent with the heart of God.

And godliness with brotherly affection. (2 Peter 1:7a)

A genuine affection for our brothers and sisters in the Body of Christ.

And brotherly affection with love. (2 Peter 1:7b)

Flowing from this aggressive walk of faith is a genuine affection for our brothers and sisters, love that has nothing to do with the character of the one being loved and everything to do with the nature of the Lover. God's selfless, poured-out love becomes visible in our relationships, and He uses that love to reveal Himself to the world.

> If these qualities are yours and are increasing, they keep you from being ineffective or unfruitful in the knowledge of our Lord Jesus Christ. (2 Peter 1:8)

As these qualities are ours and are growing within us, God continues to transform us into the image of His Son by His Holy Spirit and to pour through us the fruitfulness of His life. Peter keeps bringing us back to knowledge. Knowing God is the only valuable pursuit of the Christian life—the beginning, the end and everything in between.

MAKE YOUR CALLING AND ELECTION SURE

> Whoever lacks these qualities is so nearsighted that he is blind, having forgotten that he was cleansed from his former sins. Therefore, brothers, be all the more diligent to make your calling and election sure, for if you practice these qualities you will never fall. For in this way there will be richly provided for you an entrance into the eternal kingdom of our Lord and Savior Jesus Christ. (2 Peter 1:9-11)

Peter challenges us to be diligent and certain about God's calling and choosing us. As long as we practice these things, we will never stumble. On one hand, we need to be very careful about our brothers and sisters who have hearts that are sensitive and vulnerable to the enemy. Our enemy is continually inflicting doubts on us concerning our salvation, our relationship with God, and our ministry. At the same time, we need to be honest with one another and with the Word of God. Those who are Christ's are known by the present evidence of His life within them. Their assurance is not based on the fact that twenty years ago they raised their hand at a meeting, or they walked down an aisle or they were baptized. Those who are Christ's are always known by the fruit of His life within them.

Peter exhorts us to make our calling and election sure, to examine our relationship with God. At this point we find a wonderful promise. We remember that Jesus talked about two roads—one that was wide and led to destruction, and the other that was narrow but led to life (Matthew 7:13-14). The more we walk on the narrow road and the closer we get to the kingdom of heaven, the wider the road becomes until the gates of heaven spring open wide to welcome us as we arrive. That is an incredible hope!

The apostle Peter is picturing for us the Christian life as a process in which God develops His heart within us, His character and His life. It is a process in which we are equipped for godliness and ministry. We are not very "process-oriented" in our culture. We like our Christian life to grow to maturity in the same way we prepare our breakfast cereal: in an instant! We want to develop into strong and fruitful believers right now! We are not accustomed to "process thinking" in our western culture, but God is very process-oriented in His work. He keeps making us and re-making us; He teaches us and then re-teaches us. He develops

Adequate!

us and then develops us some more as He builds into us the heart of His Son. We are reminded once again in Peter's teaching that God is always far more concerned about the person we are along the way than anything we accomplish for Him.

OBEDIENCE THROUGH SUFFERINGS

James also talks about our walk toward growth and maturity as a process. Peter had referred to "steadfastness" or perseverance as part of God's process, and James discusses this also as he begins his letter.

> James, a servant of God and of the Lord Jesus Christ, to the twelve tribes in the Dispersion: Greetings. Count it all joy, my brothers, when you meet trials of various kinds, for you know that the testing of your faith produces steadfastness. And let steadfastness have its full effect, that you may be perfect and complete, lacking in nothing. (James 1:1-4)

As we walk in the process in which God is making us like Himself, building into us the heart of the Lord Jesus, and preparing us for ministry, perseverance will be one of the most important character qualities He would give us along the way. "Let steadfastness have its full effect," James says, "so that you will be perfect and complete, not lacking anything." James is calling us to participate with God in His process in our lives. He tells us to let it happen. Keep walking in the midst of the trials, the pain and the affliction. Do not "bail out" of the process. Endurance is one of the most important character qualities in all the Christian life.

Life is filled with a multitude of trials, and we continually meet times of testing. Temptations need to be faced and afflictions need to be borne; difficulties surface in our relationships with one another and failures often plague us. James tells us to consider these times as joyous because God is using them to develop endurance within us. He encourages us to continue with God's process during these times because He is using them to bring us to maturity. As God's sovereign process is worked out, He brings about His perfect result: a person who continues to walk with God and responds to Him even in the most difficult of trials. God's own Son learned from His Father in the very same way.

> Although he was a son, he learned obedience through what he suffered. And being made perfect, he became the source of eternal salvation to all who obey him, being designated by God a high priest after the order of Melchizedek. (Hebrews 5:8-10)

Christ was never disobedient to His Father. God was teaching His Son to continually come to Him, developing in Him a pattern of responsiveness in every situation of His life. Because Christ was willing to obey, God made Him to be the source of salvation to all who would be obedient to Him. You and I have been designated as well, not only as recipients of eternal salvation but also as His vessels through which to minister that salvation. The means God used to teach His Son is a primary tool in our lives as well. The sufferings and trials are tools that prepare chosen vessels for ministry.

Endurance is another of those things we do not know much about in our culture. We can hardly endure a headache, can we! At the first sign of any discomfort, we have all kinds of remedies to take away our pain and to make us comfortable. Though comfort is one of our most important priorities in this world, to God endurance is an even higher priority. In fact, it is one of the most important attitudes God desires to build into us. Jesus said to His disciples in Matthew 10:

You will be hated by all for my name's sake. But the one who endures to the end will be saved. (Matthew 10:22)

Discipline and Endurance

Hebrews 11, as you well know, is the passage we often refer to as
"faith's hall of fame." Faith is the major theme, however, only when
we lift out chapter 11 and make it the whole subject. When we
broaden the context from chapters 10–12, the major theme that
emerges is endurance. The writer said at the end of Hebrews 10,

You have need of endurance, so that when you have done the will
of God you may receive what is promised. (Hebrews 10:36)

In chapter 11 the author is giving us one example after another of those who through the faith God entrusted to them were
able to endure in the midst of this world. Abraham endured. He
did not allow the roots of his life to sink deeply into this system
because God had revealed to him another kingdom with a greater
depth of reality. Moses chose to endure ill treatment with the
people of God rather than to enjoy the passing pleasures of sin.
Many examples are set before us of those who endured by means
of the faith God entrusted to them.

As we come to Hebrews 12, the writer says,

Since we are surrounded by so great a cloud of witnesses, let us
also lay aside every weight, and sin which clings so closely, and
let us run with endurance the race that is set before us. (Hebrews 12:1)

The writer sets before us now the supreme example of endurance that the world had ever known, the Lord Jesus. He must fill
our vision as we run this race that ends at the very throne of God.

Looking to Jesus, the founder and perfecter of our faith, who for
the joy that was set before him endured the cross, despising the
shame, and is seated at the right hand of the throne of God. Con-

sider him who endured from sinners such hostility against him-self, so that you may not grow weary or fainthearted. In your struggle against sin you have not yet resisted to the point of shedding your blood. (Hebrews 12:2-4)

The writer now begins to discuss God's ministry of discipline that develops endurance in our lives. Endurance is the most important character quality needed to finish the race, and our Father is faithful to each of His children as He builds into us the perseverance needed to finish. He does this in the disciplines of His love.

I am so glad that the writer calls us to run with perseverance, rather than to run with speed or style or personality! This is a long distance race—not a sprint, but a marathon. It is a race that begins when we come to know Christ as our Savior and Lord, and it ends when we see His face in glory—at the very throne of God. The point of the race is to finish. What we will need more than anything else to finish this race is endurance, which is developed through discipline.

Do you understand the relationship between discipline and endurance? When we see a runner out on the track on the day of the great race, whether that is a high school track meet or the Olympics, we know that this is not the first day she has been out there on that track. Rather, she has been preparing for weeks and months, disciplining herself, so that on the day of the race she will not fall on her face before the finish line. Those months of discipline have built into her body the power needed to carry her to the end of the race and enable her to win. God disciplines us in His love to develop within us the endurance we need to finish the race and to win.

My good friend Roger is an excellent athlete. He is in such wonderful athletic condition that sometimes it is embarrassing to be around him! A few years ago, as our families were having dinner together, he began to challenge me to run with him. After he sufficiently humiliated me in front of my family, insisting that I begin a conditioning program, I said, "O.K., Roger. I'll run with you." We planned to meet at the local high school track the following Monday morning to run together.

It was a beautiful summer morning as I drove my car to the track and met Roger who had ridden his bicycle. He was already going through his warm-up exercises when I arrived. When we went onto the track he said, "OK, let's go," I took off. I was feeling so good as I poured it on. Halfway around the track I realized that I was ahead of Roger. Because I was still ahead of him at the three-quarter mark, I remember saying, "Come on, Roger, you're the runner. You are supposed to be showing me how to do this; let's go." I made up my mind I was going to finish before he did. And I did! The thing I had not realized was that Roger was planning on going around the track more than once. About the time I was completely exhausted, he was just getting into his stride. I had completely missed the point.

Sometimes we miss the point in the Christian life. The point is to finish. The most important character quality needed to finish the race is endurance. We must take hold of God and keep walking even in the midst of the pain, the loss, the disappointment and the afflictions. In this race, to finish is to win. Endurance is what we need above all else if we are to see His face at the finish line.

EVEN SATAN IS GOD'S TOOL

In God's process of developing us as vessels for the ministry of His life, Satan, our great enemy, will be one of His favorite tools. We see that in Peter's denial of his Lord.

> Simon, Simon, behold, Satan demanded to have you, that he might sift you like wheat, but I have prayed for you that your

faith may not fail. And when you have turned again, strengthen your brothers. (Luke 22:31-32)

What a graphic description this is of Satan's desire to destroy Peter on every level of his life! His enemy intended to separate him from his faith like the chaff is separated from the grain in the threshing process. We discussed earlier how God gave Satan permission to work in Job's life. Satan never could have touched him apart from His permission. This is also true of Peter, and of you and me. Peter will now face the most devastating trial of his life.

Peter must understand that he is not going to go through this alone; God is in the process with him. Jesus, our mediator, is praying for him. After Peter comes through this, he will be stronger than he was before. God will use this to develop ministry within him, and he will strengthen his brothers.

Satan is seeking to destroy us. There is no question about that; he is the enemy of our souls. However, he cannot destroy us because of God's great protecting power in the lives of His children. In his purpose to destroy us, he becomes another tool in the hands of our sovereign God as He makes us the people He has called us to be in Christ.

Do you remember what Joseph said to His brothers in the midst of that beautiful reunion? He said to those who had hated him,

As for you, you meant evil against me, but God meant it for good, to bring it about that many people should be kept alive, as they are today. (Genesis 50:20)

They had desired to destroy him, but instead they became tools in God's hands to make Joseph the man that God had called him to be and to prepare him for his ministry. That is true in our lives as well. God uses every affliction, persecution, and even Satan as tools in His process.

How does Peter respond to Jesus' encouraging assurance that he will come through this trial and be even stronger than he was before? Does he fall down at Jesus' feet and worship Him saying, "How can I thank you for preparing me for this time of devastating temptation and great trial?" Does he pour out a heart of thanksgiving of worship and praise before his Lord?

> Peter said to him, "Lord, I am ready to go with you both to prison and to death." (Luke 22:33)

Peter does not fall down in worship, humbling himself before Jesus. His flesh stands up and says, "Wait a minute, Jesus. Who are you talking about? I'm not one of those weak disciples, you know. This is Peter you're talking to! You need to know that in the darkest hour of your life, when you are alone and you are afraid, when everyone else has walked away, just remember one thing: Peter will be there. I'll go all the way with you to prison and to death."

> Jesus said, "I tell you, Peter, the rooster will not crow this day, until you deny three times that you know me." (Luke 22:34)

With all his fleshly boasts, Peter was not even able to tell that little servant girl that he belonged to Jesus. In his darkest hour, his greatest fear was realized, and he denied his Lord. He cursed and swore and said, "I never knew the man." Then he heard the cock crow, he looked up into the eyes of Jesus and went out and wept bitterly. But Jesus was in this process with Peter. He was in the process of breaking, humbling, remaking and molding. Even Peter's greatest enemy was God's most powerful tool in the process. It will be that way in our lives as well. The one who desires to destroy us becomes a tool by which God develops us, breaks us, makes us and remakes us, preparing to pour out His life through us.

THE RESERVOIR OF MINISTRY FILLED

In the beginning of Paul's second Corinthian letter, we find a wonderful passage about how God develops ministry in our hearts so that we can touch hurting people with His love.

> Paul, an apostle of Christ Jesus by the will of God, and Timothy our brother, to the church of God that is at Corinth, with all the saints who are in the whole of Achaia: Grace to you and peace from God our Father and the Lord Jesus Christ. Blessed be the God and Father of our Lord Jesus Christ, the Father of mercies and God of all comfort, (2 Corinthians 1:1-3)

I think this is my favorite description of God in all the Scriptures: "The Father of mercies and the God of all comfort." Any mercy or compassion that is ever given or received in this world comes from only one place: the heart of God. There is no mercy or comfort anywhere in this world apart from Him. He is the only source of the love that heals us, makes us whole, and sets us free.

> [He] comforts us in all our affliction, so that we may be able to comfort those who are in any affliction, with the comfort with which we ourselves are comforted by God. For as we share abundantly in Christ's sufferings, so through Christ we share abundantly in comfort too. (2 Corinthians 1:4-5)

This is a powerful picture of God's process of developing ministry in our hearts and lives. We are living in a competitive and pain-filled world in which everyone around us has far more pain in their lives than they can handle. Everywhere we look, there are people who are being crushed in the pressures of this system. Every day we are confronted with those whose circumstances are so overwhelming that they have lost all hope. There are those who are empty; all their resources are gone. God has raised us up to bring encouragement, hope and comfort to them.

What is the source of the compassion and comfort that God desires us to bring to hurting people in His name? How are the reservoirs of our hearts filled up with the things that come from the heart of God so that we can give them away to others? That is what Paul is describing here. God allows us to go through times of trials, afflictions, great pressure. As we reach out to Him for His mercy and His comfort in the midst of our pain, He pours into us those things which fill His heart. Then He brings us to people who are hurting so that we can give to them what God gave to us when we were hurting.

If we are not willing to go through this process, we will have nothing to give to hurting people. The reservoirs of our hearts are filled with the things of God in the midst of the pain of our own lives. In our afflictions and trials, we run to God and He pours Himself into us, giving us His compassion, His mercy and His comfort. Then we become a reservoir, a means by which God touches the lives of hurting people around us with the comfort of His love. Remember, the Holy Spirit who lives within us is called "the Comforter" (John 14:26, KJV).

MINISTRY: THE RESULT OF GOD'S MERCY

Paul continues his teaching about God's process in 2 Corinthians 4:

> Having this ministry by the mercy of God, we do not lose heart. (2 Corinthians 4:1)

The apostle is talking about the ministry of the new covenant that we studied in chapter 3. It is a glorious ministry, one from which flows the very life of God. It is a ministry that is lived out in great power and freedom, and one that will last forever and never fade away. Paul says, "Therefore, since through God's mercy we have this ministry." Ministry is never the result of human achievement; it is the result of God's mercy. Peter had taught us that the basis for God's call in our lives is His own glory and excellence. Paul teaches us that the foundation for ministry is His mercy.

Since through God's mercy we have this ministry, we do not lose heart. We are very prone to lose heart in ministry; even the strongest of us have great difficulty enduring. People fail to respond in the way we hope; we do not measure up to our own expectations; the enemy is continually bringing difficulties; afflictions come, persecutions confront us and we become exhausted in the midst of it all. Satan is trying to wear us down like a dog nipping at our heels. Sometimes even God does not measure up to our expectations, and we want to throw it all away. We are so vulnerable to losing heart. What is it that keeps us from losing heart in ministry? Only a "new covenant" understanding of ministry in which God becomes our strength and our adequacy, and His mercies that are new every morning. It is His mercies that keep us from losing heart, or from "burning out."

GOD PEDDLERS

Having this ministry by the mercy of God, we do not lose heart. But we have renounced disgraceful, underhanded ways. We refuse to practice cunning or to tamper with God's word, but by the open statement of the truth we would commend ourselves to everyone's conscience in the sight of God. (2 Corinthians 4:1-2)

Paul is actually returning to a theme he touched on earlier in his letter. We will go back to that also in the last few verses in chapter 2.

We are not, like so many, peddlers of God's word, but as men of sincerity, as commissioned by God, in the sight of God we speak in Christ. (2 Corinthians 2:17)

Adequate!

Though Paul is writing only thirty or thirty-five years since Jesus returned to the Father, already the "God peddlers" are on the scene! It did not take long, did it? There were those who quickly saw "ministry" as a means to personal gain. They were willing to reduce the glorious gospel of the Lord Jesus Christ to a pitch for personal profit. We are not like many peddling the Word of God. On the contrary, Paul says, "in Christ"—He is the environment for our lives and ministry. "We speak before God"—it is all open to the Father. "With sincerity"—our hearts are whole before Him. "Like men sent from God"—He is the source of our lives and ministries.

Paul is now coming back to that same theme. He says, "We renounce disgraceful, underhanded ways." Those manipulative things that are used by some people have been rejected by us. There are things we can do to cause people to respond in the flesh. There are emotional tools, manipulative methods we can use to get people to do what we want them to do. Paul says, "We've rejected those things!" We do not use deception. Our hearts are whole, pure and clear before the Lord; we are committed to the truth. We do not distort or adulterate the Word of God. We will never use the Word of God to say what we want it to say. It is not our tool to accomplish our purposes; we are the tools of the Word of God, vessels for God to use as He fulfills His purposes. The words God speaks are filled with character and integrity, and those who handle the Word of God must be filled with character and integrity as well.

A few years ago I was in Connecticut teaching a Bible conference at a local church. As I was shaving and changing clothes in preparation for the evening session, I turned on the television, thinking perhaps I could hear the news. As I turned on the TV, I found it was set on a religious station. The scene was a living room and a group of people were talking together. Just at that moment, a young woman leading the discussion said, "Now we know God promises us that when we give to Him, He will give back to us thirty, sixty and a hundredfold." I almost slit my throat with my razor! We studied that Scripture passage in the parable of the sower and the soils. God is talking about His Word multiplying within us as we hear it, accept it, and respond in obedience. But those who were broadcasting this program desired a particular response from their audience. They wanted people to send in their money. They were using the Word of God to say what they wanted it to say. Paul says, "We will never do that!" We will never, ever use the Word of God to say what we want it to say. We will not distort it; we will not adulterate it.

Paul describes his ministry as simply proclaiming the truth of God to the consciences of men and women, and trusting Him for the results. We, too, must place our confidence in the creative power of the Word of God. Only that confidence will keep us from using the Word of God as a tool for our purposes.

WE DO NOT PREACH OURSELVES

Even if our gospel is veiled, it is veiled only to those who are perishing. In their case the god of this world has blinded the minds of the unbelievers, to keep them from seeing the light of the gospel of the glory of Christ, who is the image of God. For what we proclaim is not ourselves, but Jesus Christ as Lord, with ourselves as your servants for Jesus' sake. (2 Corinthians 4:3-5)

Paul says, "We do not preach ourselves." We have not become our message! Christ is our message; the only way we will ever come to you is as your servants for His sake. How often have we heard people speak, or we have listened to programs on the radio or television, or we have read a book, and before long we realize that they are not talking about who God is and what He is doing.

They are talking about who they are and what they are doing. They have become their message.

For Paul, Christ was his message. We are not important enough to talk about. We must preach Christ and come to His people only as their servants for His sake. God uses men and women of integrity and character, with hearts like His own, to build His Church. His love is pure, His Word is true, and His character is consistent. All of His relationships are characterized by commitment. This must be true also for those whom He calls to walk with Him in ministry.

Character and integrity are always measured by the heart of a servant. There have always been two kinds of shepherds. There have been those who lay down their lives for the sheep and those who use the sheep to build their own lives. We must lay down our lives for God's people in a heart of serving.

It is interesting that Paul describes how the god of this world blinds the minds of the unbelieving. On one side he talks of those who peddle and distort the Word of God, using manipulative and deceptive means; on the other side are those who preach themselves. It could very well be that one of the primary ways that Satan blinds the minds of the unbelieving so that they might not see the gospel of Christ is by those who adulterate the Word of God, use deception and preach themselves.

How often have we had the opportunity to share our faith with people in our family, our neighborhood or at work, and we hardly even begin to get the words out when they say, "I know what you're talking about. I heard such and such a preacher on television begging for money. I don't want to hear anything about it. I'm just not interested." Satan uses the manipulations, the deceptions, the selfishness, and the preaching of ourselves to blind the minds of the unbelieving. We must walk with integrity and as servants if we are to be used of God.

TREASURE IN JARS OF CLAY

Paul says in verse 6:

> God, who said, "Let light shine out of darkness," has shone in our hearts to give the light of the knowledge of the glory of God in the face of Jesus Christ. (2 Corinthians 4:6)

Twice in history God has spoken the words, "Let there be light." Once was at the beginning of His old creation; the second time is the beginning of His new creation. In the darkness at the beginning of time, God spoke and said, "Let there be light," and the light began to shine. Even so in the darkness of our hearts God has spoken those words once again, "Let there be light," and in the darkness of our hearts the light of the gospel of Christ has begun to shine.

> We have this treasure in jars of clay, to show that the surpassing power belongs to God and not to us. (2 Corinthians 4:7)

We have this treasure, the life of Christ, the ministry of the new covenant, in earthen vessels. If you had a great treasure, what would you do with it? If you received a letter in the mail telling you that a relative you did not even know had died and left you some very valuable jewels or several ounces of gold, what would you do with them? If you did not sell them immediately, you would probably try to find the most secure place you could to keep them. What has God done? He has taken the greatest treasure the world has ever known, and He has placed it in the most fragile container the world has ever seen. God has placed the treasure of the life of His Son in you and me—common earthenware jars, so weak, so fragile, so easily broken.

Paul tells us that God has done this to prove that the power is of Himself, not of us. In the midst of our weakness, God becomes the only possible explanation for what He is doing in and through us. In this way there is no glory for us; all the glory is His. There is no question that He is the source, the power, and the means by which our lives and ministries are fulfilled. However, God not only places the life of His Son in common earthenware jars, but now He also begins to break the jars.

BROKEN VESSELS

We are afflicted in every way, but not crushed; (2 Corinthians 4:8a)

Paul tells us that in every possible way, we are afflicted. Though this may come as a great surprise to some of God's people, we really do not live in "plastic bubbles," protected from the hurtful, painful, destructive things that happen to other people in the world. The same things that happen to them happen to us. We have health and emotional problems. We have difficulties in our marriages and with our children. We experience financial pressures and struggles with our relationships in ministry. The difference with us is the result. In the world, when people are afflicted they are often crushed in the midst of the pain and pressure. We are afflicted, but we are not crushed because God is there with us providing His peace in the midst of the storms.

[We are] perplexed, but not driven to despair; (2 Corinthians 4:8b)

This is reality! Paul says, "We do not always know what is going on around us or what God's final purposes are." Have you ever gone through one of those trials and afflictions, perhaps a health crisis, an emotional crisis, or a crisis in your relationships? Sometimes in the midst of these you are suddenly surrounded by well-meaning people who all seem to be saying the same thing: "What do you think God is trying to teach you through this?" Sometimes the only honest response is, "I have absolutely no idea." Although we do not always understand what God is doing, we do not give up hope because He is there!

> [We are] persecuted, but not forsaken; struck down, but not destroyed; (2 Corinthians 4:9)

We may be persecuted, but we are never forsaken because God's presence remains with us. The Holy Spirit will never leave us. We may be struck down, but we will never be destroyed because He is our keeper.

> [We are] always carrying in the body the death of Jesus, so that the life of Jesus may also be manifested in our bodies. (2 Corinthians 4:10)

Paul begins to describe now how life and death are working simultaneously within us. In our physical bodies, we carry with us the death of Jesus. But even in our dying, His life is revealed in us.

GOD'S LIFE RELEASED

> We who live are always being given over to death for Jesus' sake, so that the life of Jesus also may be manifested in our mortal flesh. So death is at work in us, but life in you. (2 Corinthians 4:11-12)

Paul tells us that God is continually bringing us into situations in which we die so that His life may be revealed in our mortal bodies. "Death is working in us, but life is at work in you." Paul goes on to say that God is bringing us into situations in which we come to the end of ourselves so that His life is released through us to those around us. Our afflictions and persecutions are part of God's process of bringing His ministry to others. As

Adequate!

His life pours out of us to them, ministry is fulfilled. Ministry is the overflow of the life of God as we walk with Him. In the process of our dying and laying down of our lives, He pours His life through us to others. Unless we are willing to come to the end of ourselves and to endure in the afflictions, there will be no release of His life to transform others and to give them hope. Ministry takes place in the process of our dying.

> We do not lose heart. Though our outer nature is wasting away, our inner nature is being renewed day by day. For this slight momentary affliction is preparing for us an eternal weight of glory beyond all comparison, as we look not to the things that are seen but to the things that are unseen. For the things that are seen are transient, but the things that are unseen are eternal. (2 Corinthians 4:16-18)

We do not give up hope in this process of dying, because even as our outer person is breaking down, God is continually giving life to our inner person. Because God has given us an eternal perspective, we see these afflictions and sufferings as only temporary and light in relation to the way in which God is using them to develop within us a ministry which will last for all eternity.

Paul is contrasting two kinds of "ministry" in these verses: one that can be peddled and marketed, and the other that releases the very life of God. There is a fleshly thing some call ministry which offers what people will buy. It is characterized by deception and manipulation. It adulterates the Word of God and uses the people of God to build personal kingdoms. However, God uses genuine ministry to pour out His own life at the cost of our lives.

A BROKEN PROPHET

I would like to look with you further in the Scriptures at this picture of the treasure and the vessel; how God releases His life

through the breaking of the vessel. Jeremiah's life and ministry again become a vivid picture of what God desires to teach
us.

> Thus says the LORD, "Go, buy a potter's earthenware flask, and
> take some of the elders of the people and some of the elders of the
> priests, and go out to the Valley of the Son of Hinnom at the entry
> of the Potsherd Gate, and proclaim there the words that I tell
> you. You shall say, 'Hear the word of the LORD, O kings of Judah
> and inhabitants of Jerusalem. Thus says the LORD of hosts, the
> God of Israel: Behold, I am bringing such disaster upon this
> place that the ears of everyone who hears of it will tingle.'"
> (Jeremiah 19:1-3)

God's anger had grown toward His hard-hearted, rebellious
people. Their religious leaders expressed no heart of submission
to the Lord; they ruled on their own authority. God was preparing
an "object lesson" for them through His prophet Jeremiah. He
would break His people, even as one breaks a potter's vessel.

> Because the people have forsaken me and have profaned this
> place by making offerings in it to other gods whom neither they
> nor their fathers nor the kings of Judah have known; and be-
> cause they have filled this place with the blood of innocents, and
> have built the high places of Baal to burn their sons in the fire as
> burnt offerings to Baal, which I did not command or decree, nor
> did it come into my mind (Jeremiah 19:4-5)

I do not think we can even begin to sense the anger and the
pain that fill the heart of God at this place. We can almost hear
Him saying to His people, "I knew that you would be depraved; I
knew that you would be rebellious; I knew that you would be
hard-hearted, but it never even entered my mind that you would
take your own sons and daughters and burn them in the fires of
sacrifice to Baal." As we read this, we must be gripped with how

Adequate!

God feels about our modern form of child sacrifice, with the scourge of abortion murdering millions of children each year.

> Behold, days are coming, declares the LORD, when this place shall no more be called Topheth, or the Valley of the Son of Hinnom, but the Valley of Slaughter. (Jeremiah 19:6)

Topheth, the valley of Ben Hinnom, was a place of burning. It would now be known as a place of slaughter, as God would judge His people.

God had told Jeremiah to take a potter's vessel to the senior priests and warn them of God's coming judgment. Now he was instructed to break the jar.

> You shall break the flask in the sight of the men who go with you, and shall say to them, "Thus says the LORD of hosts: So will I break this people and this city, as one breaks a potter's vessel, so that it can never be mended. Men shall bury in Topheth because there will be no place else to bury. Thus will I do to this place, declares the LORD, and to its inhabitants, making this city like Topheth." (Jeremiah 19:10-12)

How do the people of God receive Jeremiah's message? How do they respond when the prophet brings to them the Word God had entrusted to him?

> Pashhur the priest, the son of Immer, who was chief officer in the house of the LORD, heard Jeremiah prophesying these things. Then Pashhur beat Jeremiah the prophet, and put him in the stocks that were in the upper Benjamin Gate of the house of the LORD. (Jeremiah 20:1-2)

How did the religious leaders respond to the prophetic message God had entrusted to Jeremiah? Did they come to Jeremiah and say, "Please go back to God and ask for mercy. Ask Him to be patient with us, to give us time so that we can call a fast. Let us bring all the people to Him with whole hearts of repentance.

Please go back to God and ask for time to repent." There is no response of brokenness to this message. Instead, they try to break the messenger. The chief priests had Jeremiah beaten and put in stocks at the city gate so that as people walked back and forth, they could look at him and laugh.

This is more than Jeremiah can handle. He begins to pour out his disappointment, his confusion and his anger before the Lord. We can hardly comprehend the bitterness his words represent.

> O LORD, you have deceived me, and I was deceived; you are stronger than I, and you have prevailed. I have become a laughingstock all the day; everyone mocks me. For whenever I speak, I cry out, I shout, "Violence and destruction!" For the word of the LORD has become for me a reproach and derision all day long. (Jeremiah 20:7-8)

Jeremiah begins to pour out his heart to God and says, "God, you lied to me." We could almost visualize lightning coming out of the sky and striking Jeremiah dead! He is accusing God of deception! "God, You told me to take this flask to the leaders of the people and tell them that just as one breaks this potter's vessel in a way that it cannot be repaired, that is what you are going to do to this city. You did not do it. You did not break the city; you broke me instead. What you say you will do to the people has not happened. These people are not hurting. They express no pain for their sin; they continue in their old rebellious ways. There is no affliction, no ridicule for them. What you say you are going to do to the people, you do not do. You do it to me instead!" Jeremiah is saying, "I've had it!" Later on in this lament he says, "I'm sorry I was ever born." That expresses Jeremiah's heart toward the Lord.

Can God handle this? Can God openly receive the honest and deep cries of our hearts? The most beautiful thing about Jeremiah's lament is that it is a prayer. Jeremiah is bringing all his anguish to the God who can handle the pains of our lives and all that is in our hearts. We need to bring it all to Him. Our Father can receive our honesty in the midst of our pain. He bears with us rather than destroying us.

A FIRE IN MY BONES

God said He would break the people, and instead Jeremiah is the one who is broken again and again. This was the pattern of his ministry. But what else does Jeremiah say?

> If I say, "I will not mention him, or speak any more in his name," there is in my heart as it were a burning fire shut up in my bones, and I am weary with holding it in, and I cannot. (Jeremiah 20:9)

What a situation to be in! If Jeremiah speaks the Word of God, he is beaten, put into the stocks and ridiculed. If he does not speak the Word of God, he cannot hold it in. It is like a fire in his bones. What a picture this is of the treasure and the vessel! Even as the vessel is being broken, the treasure, the life of God within him, is growing and flowing. It is being released even in his brokenness.

TORCHES, TRUMPETS, AND BROKEN JARS

We talked about Gideon earlier in our study. For seven years the people of God had been oppressed and afflicted by the Midianites. As their hearts became enslaved by the gods of their enemies, God allowed them to become physical captives as well. It seemed that the only way for them to learn was for God to mirror their inner condition with their physical circumstances. Year after year this was the pattern of their lives. However, God in His mercy heard their cry for deliverance and provided a man for that ministry: Gideon.

The Midianites had a great army of 135,000 soldiers. Gideon finally realized that God was calling him to be the champion of His people, and that God would use him even with his weaknesses and lack of faith. God met him graciously in his fears and strengthened his faith. When Gideon got his army together, he had only 32,000 soldiers to fight 135,000 of the enemy! Do you remember what God said to Gideon?

> The LORD said to Gideon, "The people with you are too many for me to give the Midianites into their hand, lest Israel boast over me, saying, 'My own hand has saved me.' Now therefore proclaim in the ears of the people, saying, 'Whoever is fearful and trembling, let him return home and hurry away from Mount Gilead.'" Then 22,000 of the people returned, and 10,000 remained. (Judges 7:2-3)

How many battles do you think there have been in history in which the general stood up before the army the day before the battle and said, "Is anyone here afraid? Just go on home." Twenty-two thousand men went home, so that Gideon now had 10,000 soldiers to fight 135,000. In God's eyes, this was still too many.

> The LORD said to Gideon, "The people are still too many. Take them down to the water, and I will test them for you there, and anyone of whom I say to you, 'This one shall go with you,' shall go with you, and anyone of whom I say to you, 'This one shall not go with you,' shall not go." So he brought the people down to the water. And the LORD said to Gideon, "Every one who laps the water with his tongue, as a dog laps, you shall set by himself. Likewise, every one who kneels down to drink." And the number of those who lapped, putting their hands to their mouths, was 300 men, but all the rest of the people knelt down to drink water. (Judges 7:4-6)

Adequate!

Then God said something amazing to Gideon! This battle would be won in a way that His power and glory would be displayed.

> The LORD said to Gideon, "With the 300 men who lapped I will save you and give the Midianites into your hand, and let all the others go every man to his home." (Judges 7:7)

There were further encouragements to Gideon's faith and plans for the battle laid. Before they went out to meet the enemy Gideon divided his band of three hundred men into three companies. He placed in each man's hands trumpets and empty jars filled with torches. He then gave them the battle strategy:

> Gideon and the hundred men who were with him came to the outskirts of the camp at the beginning of the middle watch, when they had just set the watch. And they blew the trumpets and smashed the jars that were in their hands. Then the three companies blew the trumpets and broke the jars. They held in their left hands the torches, and in their right hands the trumpets to blow. And they cried out, "A sword for the LORD and for Gideon!" Every man stood in his place around the camp, and all the army ran. They cried out and fled. (Judges 7:19-21)

They surrounded the enemy, heard the cry, blew the trumpets, and broke the pitchers. When the jars were broken, the light of the torches was released. The enemy destroyed themselves and a great victory was won.

> When they blew the 300 trumpets, the LORD set every man's sword against his comrade and against all the army. And the army fled as far as Beth-shittah toward Zererah, as far as the border of Abel-meholah, by Tabbath. (Judges 7:22)

This same picture fills Scripture. God develops ministry within us in the midst of our afflictions. He pours His life into us as we turn to Him in our weakness and our pain. It is then in the breaking of the vessel that the treasure of His life is released. This is God's process for developing and pouring out ministry. Death works in us, and life in others. It is not possible to remove the reality of the cross from the nature of ministry.

This has always been God's way to ministry. That is the way it was for Gideon, for Jeremiah, and for the Lord Jesus. "The fullness of deity in bodily form" (Colossians 2:9) came into this world filled with the life of God. The vessel was broken, and God's life was released to us. That is the way it was for the apostle Paul and for Jim Elliot and his brothers in Ecuador as they sought to reach the Auca Indians. That is the way it was for Chester Bitterman, and that is the way it will be for you and me. God will release His life through us in the breaking of the vessel, in the laying down of our lives. May God give us the grace to seek the ministry that releases His life, even if it does not "sell" in the eyes of this world.

QUESTIONS FOR COMMUNICATION AND APPLICATION

1. Do you see God developing in you the qualities listed in 2 Peter? Where are you the strongest? the weakest?

2. Where have you seen God give you His comfort in the midst of suffering and affliction? Have you seen Him use this as a basis for ministering in the lives of others?

3. How do you respond to the suffering and afflictions God is using to break down your outer person? How do you see Him expressing Himself more powerfully during these times when you are weak?

4. Do you have the freedom to be honest with God in your times of hurt and depression? Are you able to be real before God and people?

And so, from the day we heard, we have not ceased to pray for you, asking that you may be filled with the knowledge of his will in all spiritual wisdom and understanding,

Colossians 1:9

5

Striving for One Another's Faith

We have been talking in our study about ministry as "what God does." He is not looking for people who will do great things for Him. God is looking for those through whom He can fulfill His eternal works. He moves us to walk with Him by filling our eyes and our hearts with His beauty, compels us through the love of His Son and gives us responsive hearts by His Spirit. We see this truth modeled so clearly, so visibly and so powerfully in the ministry of the Lord Jesus. He did not speak one word nor fulfill one work of His own. The Father's initiative was the source, the Father's power was the means and the Father's glory was the end for all that Jesus did. He is not only our model for ministry but also the power through which ministry is fulfilled. "Christ in you, the hope of glory" is the key to all our lives and ministries.

We also talked about the "new covenant relationship" in which our sufficiency and adequacy no longer come from us, but from God. We have looked at how the Word of God is His tool for ministry; God is actually able to create life in the hearts of people by means of the words He speaks. We have also seen something of God's process of developing us as vessels for the ministry of His life, using even our failures, the afflictions of this life and Satan as His tool.

As we continue, we want to encourage you to pray. Prayer underlies all ministry and is the environment in which we respond to God. Prayer is the relationship in which God builds His heart into us and gives us direction for ministry through the Holy Spirit.

Every one of us struggles with our prayer lives. Whether we battle with business, laziness, fear of intimacy, or lack of desire, we all know that our time and intensity in prayer are greatly lacking. But our heavenly Father continually woos us to this intimate communion relationship with Him.

It overwhelms our hearts that our sovereign Creator with His vast eternal attributes would desire to communicate with creatures made out of dust. It is even more amazing that He would allow us to have power in our prayer relationship with Him. However, He invites us to come to Him, learn His mind, respond to Him and participate with Him in the work He is doing in this world, especially in the lives of our brothers and sisters in Christ.

A COMMUNION RELATIONSHIP

We see these wonderful truths in Abraham's prayer for the cities of Sodom and Gomorrah.

> The men set out from there, and they looked down toward Sodom. And Abraham went with them to set them on their way. (Genesis 18:16)

The men Moses refers to here are the angels God had sent to look at the cities. Through these messengers, God would observe the depravity of this place.

The LORD said, "Shall I hide from Abraham what I am about to do, seeing that Abraham shall surely become a great and mighty nation, and all the nations of the earth shall be blessed in him? For I have chosen him, that he may command his children and his household after him to keep the way of the LORD by doing righteousness and justice, so that the LORD may bring to Abraham what he has promised him." (Genesis 18:17-19)

Abraham had been sovereignly chosen by God to raise up a people of faithfulness to Himself. Because of Abraham's calling and the relationship of intimacy that God privileged him to share, He desired to reveal His Person and His purposes to His friend.

The LORD said, "Because the outcry against Sodom and Gomorrah is great and their sin is very grave, I will go down to see whether they have done altogether according to the outcry that has come to me. And if not, I will know." So the men turned from there and went toward Sodom, but Abraham still stood before the LORD. Then Abraham drew near and said, "Will you indeed sweep away the righteous with the wicked?" (Genesis 18:20-23)

Abraham begins his prayer with a sense of confrontation before the Lord. He seems almost to be assuming in his prayer that God will do something outside of His character in His dealing with Sodom and Gomorrah. Would God actually sweep away the righteous with the wicked?

"Suppose there are fifty righteous within the city. Will you then sweep away the place and not spare it for the fifty righteous who are in it? Far be it from you to do such a thing, to put the righteous to death with the wicked, so that the righteous fare as the wicked! Far be that from you! Shall not the Judge of all the earth do what is just?" (Genesis 18:24-25)

This is an amazing picture! A creature of dust is calling the Lord God, the One who reigns forever and ever, to justice.

> The LORD said, "If I find at Sodom fifty righteous in the city, I will spare the whole place for their sake." (Genesis 18:26)

God in His wonderful, divine humility does not look at Abraham and say, "What right do you have to talk to me about my justice?" He responds in gentleness and compassion to Abraham's heart and to his request.

> Abraham answered and said, "Behold, I have undertaken to speak to the Lord, I who am but dust and ashes. Suppose five of the fifty righteous are lacking. Will you destroy the whole city for lack of five?" And he said, "I will not destroy it if I find forty-five there." Again he spoke to him and said, "Suppose forty are found there." He answered, "For the sake of forty I will not do it." Then he said, "Oh let not the Lord be angry, and I will speak. Suppose thirty are found there." He answered, "I will not do it, if I find thirty there." (Genesis 18:27-30)

As Abraham is praying, we sense his apprehension. His desire that God's justice be revealed is so great, and at the same time his concern for the cities of Sodom and Gomorrah is genuine. Yet, he sees himself properly as a finite creature, a man made of dust, in relationship to an infinite God who rules in sovereignty over His creation.

> He said, "Behold, I have undertaken to speak to the Lord. Suppose twenty are found there." He answered, "For the sake of twenty I will not destroy it." Then he said, "Oh let not the Lord be angry, and I will speak again but this once. Suppose ten are found there." He answered, "For the sake of ten I will not destroy it." And the LORD went his way, when he had finished speaking to Abraham, and Abraham returned to his place. (Genesis 18:31-33)

I love the way the King James translation renders that last verse:

The LORD went His way, as soon as He had left communing with Abraham: and Abraham returned unto his place. (Genesis 18:33, KJV)

This rendering of the text is so revealing. As we visualize this scene, do we see Abraham convincing God to do something He would really rather not do? Is Abraham's persistence wearing God down, so that God finally gives in out of weariness? It is interesting that Abraham stopped praying at ten. We do not know whether he thought he could not talk God into sparing the city for fewer than ten people. Perhaps he was just giving up inside as he was being reminded of the devastating depravity of these cities. Do you remember how many people God brought out of the city before He destroyed it? He saved four—Lot, his wife and their two daughters. Abraham stopped praying at ten and God redeemed four. We might even see a contrast of values here. Did Abraham think that God would not be willing to spare the cities for fewer than ten people? God's heart of compassion was revealed in His redemption of Lot's family.

God was communing with Abraham. We have a God who seeks intimacy and who desires communion with His people. We see that desire revealed throughout the Scriptures when He walked in the garden in the cool of the day with Adam and then when He pursued Adam and Eve when they were hiding in the trees in the midst of their sin. When we were cut off from God because of our sin, God pursued us all the way to the cross where through the death of the Lord Jesus, the veil of the temple was torn in two from the top to the bottom, and God invited us into His very presence. God desires communion; He hungers for intimacy with His people.

The description we have of Abraham's prayer for Sodom and Gomorrah is not one of his wearing God down, of convincing God that He ought to act differently than His purposes. Abraham is reflecting back to God His heart in prayer. In the communion of prayer, God has been building His own heart into Abraham; He has been giving Abraham His compassion for people. Abraham was not this kind of man when God found him. He was an idol worshiper who came from a family of idol worshipers. God did not call Abraham to be the father of the faithful because of his personal righteousness; he was a heathen when God found him. But in the communion of prayer, God has been making Abraham's heart like His own. As Abraham brings back to God His own heart in prayer, his prayer becomes a prayer of great power.

THE HEART OF A SHEPHERD

We see this truth in Moses' prayer for the people of God after the incident of the golden calf. Moses had spent forty days in communion with God, and in Exodus 33 his hunger for the Lord had grown to the degree that he desired to see God's face. Moses is angry at the rebellion of God's people, but God's own anger is revealed to His servant Moses in a fury which His people and we must see.

> The LORD said to Moses, "Go down, for your people, whom you brought up out of the land of Egypt, have corrupted themselves. They have turned aside quickly out of the way that I commanded them. They have made for themselves a golden calf and have worshiped it and sacrificed to it and said, 'These are your gods, O Israel, who brought you up out of the land of Egypt!'" (Exodus 32:7-8)

I read this and think of a family in which the husband or wife is away for a while, perhaps just one day at work or a few days of business or visiting family. While one partner is gone, the children are disobedient and rebellious. The partner who is home becomes frustrated and worn down. When the other returns, one of the first things said is, "Let me tell you what your children were like while you were gone." The one who has come home may respond, "Wait a minute. All of a sudden these are my children? I thought they were our children." I wonder if that is how Moses felt here. The Lord said to Moses, "Go down because *your* people, whom *you* brought up out of Egypt have become corrupt." I can almost hear Moses say, "Wait a minute. All of a sudden these are my people? I thought they were your people."

> They have turned aside quickly out of the way that I commanded them. They have made for themselves a golden calf and have worshiped it and sacrificed to it and said, "These are your gods, O Israel, who brought you up out of the land of Egypt!" (Exodus 32:8)

Once again, I do not think we can begin to sense the anger and pain that must fill God's heart. He had delivered them from their enemies and their slavery by the power of His own hand, and now His people are falling before a calf of gold and saying, "This is the God, O Israel, who brought you from the land of Egypt."

> The LORD said to Moses, "I have seen this people, and behold, it is a stiff-necked people. Now therefore let me alone, that my wrath may burn hot against them and I may consume them, in order that I may make a great nation of you." (Exodus 32:9-10)

God is making an amazing offer to Moses. Although we know that Abraham is the father of all the faithful, God is talking of destroying His people, starting over with Moses, and raising up a people who will walk before Him in obedience. How grateful we are that Moses was more committed to God and His purposes than he was to his own reputation!

153

Moses implored the LORD his God and said, "O LORD, why does your wrath burn hot against your people, whom you have brought out of the land of Egypt with great power and with a mighty hand? Why should the Egyptians say, 'With evil intent did he bring them out, to kill them in the mountains and to consume them from the face of the earth'? Turn from your burning anger and relent from this disaster against your people. Remember Abraham, Isaac, and Israel, your servants, to whom you swore by your own self, and said to them, 'I will multiply your offspring as the stars of heaven, and all this land that I have promised I will give to your offspring, and they shall inherit it forever.'" And the LORD relented from the disaster that he had spoken of bringing on his people. (Exodus 32:11-14)

WHO CHANGES WHEN WE PRAY?

What is taking place in this incredible scene before us? Who changes when we pray? Can we be grateful that Moses just happened to be on the scene when God was about to lose control of Himself in His anger? That Moses was there to place his hand on God's shoulder and say, "God, maybe you ought to count to ten before you do something that you will regret later." Who changes when we pray? Where did Moses get the heart that he is now bringing back to God in prayer, a heart that reflects God's own commitment to His people?

Is this the heart we see in Moses at the burning bush when God called him? Did Moses respond to God by saying, "At last, you are showing some compassion for your enslaved people! I have been out here in the wilderness for years praying and praying that you would express some concern for them"? Absolutely not. Moses had no heart for God or for His people. He showed very little interest in being a part of God's deliverance ministry. But in the time that God and Moses had been walking together, in the communion they were sharing, God had been building His heart into Moses. As Moses prays, he is bringing back to God the heart of God, and it becomes a prayer of great power. God is allowing Moses to participate with Him in the working out of His will in the lives of His people. God transforms our hearts in the communion of prayer; as we bring back to God His heart in prayer, we participate powerfully in the work He is doing.

As Moses prayed for God's people the next day, asking God to forgive them, we see the heart of God reflected even more fully.

> The next day Moses said to the people, "You have sinned a great sin. And now I will go up to the LORD; perhaps I can make atonement for your sin." So Moses returned to the LORD and said, "Alas, this people have sinned a great sin. They have made for themselves gods of gold. But now, if you will forgive their sin—but if not, please blot me out of your book that you have written." (Exodus 32:30-32)

Moses came to the Lord seeking forgiveness and compassion for God's people, saying, "God, if you cannot forgive them, remove my name from the book you have written." This man, who had no heart for Him or for His people when God found him hiding in the wilderness, now has a heart so much like his Father's that he says, "God, take my life in their place." He is willing to lay down his life for the people of God. Thus it will be for you and me. God builds His heart into us as we commune with Him in prayer.

Prayer is not "punching a cosmic computer," and if we press all the right buttons in the right order we receive that for which we are asking. Prayer is not badgering God until, out of weariness, He gives into us. Prayer is not talking ourselves into believing so that God can honor our faith. Prayer is not in any way something we do that gets results from God. Prayer is communing with Him. In the intimacy our Father allows us to share with Him, He transforms us and gives us His heart. As we reflect to

God His own heart, prayer becomes powerful. We are changed when we pray.

When we pray for one another, we become part of an eternal team! In his letter to the church at Rome, the apostle Paul taught us of Jesus' present ministry of interceding for us before His Father. When we pray for family members, pastors and leaders, brothers and sisters who are suffering persecution, or those whom God has entrusted to us in ministry, we join with Him.

> Who shall bring any charge against God's elect? It is God who justifies. Who is to condemn? Christ Jesus is the one who died—more than that, who was raised—who is at the right hand of God, who indeed is interceding for us. (Romans 8:33-34)

Paul taught us also about the ministry of the Holy Spirit in his Roman letter. One of His primary ministries on our behalf is that of intercession.

> The Spirit helps us in our weakness. For we do not know what to pray for as we ought, but the Spirit himself intercedes for us with groanings too deep for words. And he who searches hearts knows what is the mind of the Spirit, because the Spirit intercedes for the saints according to the will of God. (Romans 8:26-27)

Even the most mature and godly of God's children do not know how to pray, as we ought to pray. Our understandings are limited and our motives and our flesh taints desires. We do not see the Father's purposes clearly. We are grateful that God searches our hearts, and the Holy Spirit intercedes for us according to the Father's will. In prayer for one another, we are joining with the Father, Son and Holy Spirit as we intercede for them.

We are powerfully reminded here of the great wonder and mystery of prayer. Our sovereign God never changes. He will fulfill every purpose of His heart. We cannot add anything to what

God is doing, and yet He invites us into His purposes, calling us to participate with Him in great power as He works out His will in the lives of those we love.

THE KNOWLEDGE OF HIS WILL

We see another aspect of prayer in Paul's ministry of intercession. Prayer is not only an intimate communion relationship in which God makes us like Himself and gives us His heart; it is also a relationship in which He privileges us to strive with Him for the faith of those whom He has entrusted to us in ministry.

> From the day we heard, we have not ceased to pray for you, asking that you may be filled with the knowledge of his will in all spiritual wisdom and understanding, so as to walk in a manner worthy of the Lord, fully pleasing to him, bearing fruit in every good work and increasing in the knowledge of God. May you be strengthened with all power, according to his glorious might, for all endurance and patience with joy, giving thanks to the Father, who has qualified you to share in the inheritance of the saints in light. (Colossians 1:9-12)

This is an amazing prayer from the apostle Paul. As we read his prayer, we sense that the things Paul is asking God to do in the midst of the church at Colossae are surely the same things God must desire to do in that place. When Paul asks that his brothers and sisters might be filled with the knowledge of God's will and live a life worthy of Him, to bear fruit and grow in knowledge, to be strengthened with power and express great endurance, and to joyously give thanks to the Father, we know that Paul is praying for his brothers and sisters at Colossae the very things God wants to do among His people in that place.

One amazing reality about this text is that Paul had never been to Colossae! He did not know these people personally, yet he

157

prays with such intimate knowledge about them and their needs. Paul must have come before the Lord continually with a listening, sensitive, responsive heart and said, "God, would you open my eyes to see the church at Colossae the way you see it? Would you cause my heart to be sensitive to their needs? What is it that you desire to do in their midst?" Those were the very things, then, that Paul brought back to God in prayer. He also took his ministry of prayer a step further when he wrote a letter to the church at Colossae, telling them the very things he was asking God to do in their midst.

This is a wonderful pattern for our prayer lives. If we are teaching a Sunday school class, leading a Bible study, or pastoring a church, if we have a ministry of counseling or of leadership in the church, how do we know what God desires to do in the lives of our people? Jesus said earlier in our study:

> ..."Truly, truly, I say to you, the Son can do nothing of his own accord, but only what he sees the Father doing. For whatever the Father does, that the Son does likewise. For the Father loves the Son and shows him all that he himself is doing. And greater works than these will he show him, so that you may marvel." (John 5:19-20)

This must be true in our ministries also. We must be doing what we see God doing. How does God give us eyes to see what He is doing? As we are involved in ministries, can we trust in our own intuition or our own abilities to discern what needs must be met in the lives of those whom God has given to us? If we could discern these needs on our own, we would have a basis on which to place tremendous confidence in ourselves. But we cannot discern the needs of people by means of our own resources. Like Paul, we need to come to our Father with a sensitive heart and say, "God, would you open my eyes to see these people the way you see them? Cause my heart to be sensitive to their needs. What do you want to do in their lives; how can you use me among them?" Those, then, are the things we must bring back to God in prayer.

Our prayer ministries can then be taken a step further. Like Paul did, we can write to people and share what we are asking God to do in their lives. Have you ever received a letter like that? If you have, you have never forgotten it. I am not talking here about a quick note that says, "I'm praying for you," but about others sharing with you specifically what they are asking God to do in your life. "I am praying that in the midst of this great pain and hurt our Father's mercies and comfort will be yours today. I am praying that in the face of these devastating circumstances, our Father will supply everything you need each day out of His riches in glory in Christ Jesus. May God strengthen you by His Spirit and give you His grace to endure in the midst of these pressures. I am asking God to keep your heart in the face of these problems. I am praying that God will heal the broken places in your relationships."

What a ministry of life to God's people! From this amazing pattern in Paul's ministry, we can follow his example in our own ministry of intercession for our prayer lives. I encourage you to do that. First come to God and ask Him to open your eyes to see people the way He sees them and to cause your heart to be sensitive to their needs. Then bring those very things back to God in a ministry of intercession, as Paul did. Follow his example, too, by sharing with people the way in which you are praying for them.

THE EYES OF YOUR HEART ENLIGHTENED

Because I have heard of your faith in the Lord Jesus and your love toward all the saints, I do not cease to give thanks for you, remembering you in my prayers, that the God of our Lord Jesus

Adequate!

> Christ, the Father of glory, may give you a spirit of wisdom and of
> revelation in the knowledge of him, (Ephesians 1:15-17)

Hearing about God's great work among the Ephesian brothers and sisters caused Paul's heart to continually overflow with
thanksgiving before the Lord. He was reminded again and again
to ask God to enable His children in Ephesus to know Him better.
We see this pattern again in the verses that follow, to pray that

> having the eyes of your hearts enlightened, that you may know
> what is the hope to which he has called you, what are the riches
> of his glorious inheritance in the saints, and what is the immea-
> surable greatness of his power toward us who believe, according
> to the working of his great might that he worked in Christ when
> he raised him from the dead and seated him at his right hand in
> the heavenly places, far above all rule and authority and power
> and dominion, and above every name that is named, not only in
> this age but also in the one to come. (Ephesians 1:18-21)

How often Paul's prayers merge with his teaching! Filling his
letters are prayers of worship, praise, spiritual warfare,
thanksgiving, and intercession for the needs of his brothers and
sisters.

As we read this prayer, we sense once again that what Paul is
asking God to do in the church at Ephesus surely must be the
very things God desires to do in their midst. Paul asked for a
spirit of wisdom and revelation among the people of God, that the
eyes of their hearts might be enlightened, that God's people
might know the hope which comes only from Him, and for the
glories of His inheritance. Paul expressed his great desire that
God's people might know Him. These are the bases for Paul's
prayer for God's people. He must have come before the Lord with
a sensitive, listening heart and asked God to enable him to see
the church at Ephesus through His eyes, and then he brought

those things back to God in prayer. This is a ministry of intercession which participates with God in a powerful way in the outworking of His will among His people. Paul's prayer life is a vivid example for us as we, too, intercede on behalf of those whom God has entrusted to us. This is a strong encouragement for us to intercede in this way before the Lord on behalf of our husband or wife, our children and our leaders.

PRAYER AND SPIRITUAL WARFARE

> Finally, be strong in the Lord and in the strength of his might. Put on the whole armor of God, that you may be able to stand against the schemes of the devil. For we do not wrestle against flesh and blood, but against the rulers, against the authorities, against the cosmic powers over this present darkness, against the spiritual forces of evil in the heavenly places. (Ephesians 6:10-12)

Satan desires to convince us that our battles are against flesh and blood and that if we could just convince people of the truth, if we could just persuade them to move toward God, if we could grip hold of their hearts and move them to trust Christ as their Savior, or if we could surround them with our love and keep them in the direction they ought to go, the battles would be won. No, our battles are not against flesh and blood, not our will against their will, not our understanding against their lack of understanding, not our eloquence against their stubbornness. Our battles are against the rulers and authorities of this dark world. Resources that come from us make absolutely no difference in spiritual wars. This is why Paul says

> Take up the whole armor of God, that you may be able to withstand in the evil day, and having done all, to stand firm. (Ephesians 6:13)

Adequate!

This is a wonderful promise for the people of God! We have talked considerably about endurance and about afflictions and temptations and about how our enemy is seeking to destroy us. We look around us in this world and see everything continually moving and shifting. There is very little stability, very little to be sure about in this world. For us, for our children, and for those whom God has given to us in ministry, this is a great promise. Even in this kind of world we can stand firm! For us there is great stability and sureness because we find our lives in God and stand strong in who He is.

Paul continues by teaching us about the specific pieces of armor—the belt of truth, the breastplate of righteousness, the gospel of peace on our feet, the shield of faith, the helmet of salvation, and the sword of the spirit, and he encourages them to be

> praying at all times in the Spirit, with all prayer and supplication. To that end keep alert with all perseverance, making supplication for all the saints, and also for me, that words may be given to me in opening my mouth boldly to proclaim the mystery of the gospel, for which I am an ambassador in chains, that I may declare it boldly, as I ought to speak. (Ephesians 6:18-20)

Prayer is the most significant aspect of the armor of God! Paul had begun the letter by sharing how he was praying for his brothers and sisters in Ephesus. He closes by asking them to pray for him. After calling them to be on the alert in prayer for all the saints, he asks them to pray that God would give him boldness in ministry.

What does this teach us about the Bible study we are leading, the church we are pastoring, or the home group we are facilitating? What does this tell us about our family ministries? How confident are we that we can discern what must happen in the lives of these people, and that we have the answers for their questions and the persuasiveness to move them? We look at the temptations our people are facing, the enemy who is seeking to destroy them, and the world that is seeking to consume them. How confident are we that we have the resources needed for ministry? We realize that our resources run out quickly and we fall on our faces in prayer. Those of us who have children know that there is nothing like parenting teenagers to teach us to pray. Those who have businesses that are struggling know that there is nothing like a business failure to teach us to pray. The pain we may experience in our marriage or our churches also causes us to fall on our faces before the Lord.

When we are in desperate need, we run to the Lord in prayer. Sometimes we live with the illusion that we need to learn how to pray in order to "do it right." We often even misquote this familiar text in Luke:

> Now Jesus was praying in a certain place, and when he finished, one of his disciples said to him, "Lord, teach us to pray, as John taught his disciples." (Luke 11:1)

We often add a word to this verse, because we know that the disciples were really asking Jesus to teach them *how* to pray. For too many of us, the proper method is always the answer. We are confident that if someone will teach us the proper principles and methods, we can accomplish what needs to be done. But we do not need to be taught how to pray. We need to be taught to pray, to run to our Father in every situation with the cries of our hearts and the burdens of our lives.

STRATEGIC PRAYER

We are looking at strategic prayer and spiritual warfare. In spiritual warfare, prayer is the way the enemy is defeated. Paul is de-

163

scribing in these passages how our battles against the forces of wickedness in the heavenly places are won. Nothing that comes from us can make any difference in the face of demonic hosts or strongholds that must be destroyed. That is why we are called to prayer. In prayer we participate with God in a powerful way in the working out of His will and in owning the victories that were won on the cross of Calvary. Strategic prayer is spiritual warfare.

I remember when Karen and I were faced with parenting our sons in the middle of their teenage years. How quickly we realized how little we could say to them anymore! When we saw what they were facing every day in this world, we learned to pray in a new way. We would fall on our faces before the Lord and cry out, "God, would you surround Peter and Joel with your angels as they go out into this world today? Would you keep their hearts for yourself? Would you stimulate within them a hunger to be men of God? Would you give them a desire to know you? Would you give them a love for you that consumes every other passion in their lives? God, would you prepare them for the building of your church?" What could we have said to move them in that way? Prayer is spiritual warfare in which we are battling against the forces of wickedness in the heavenly realms and participating with God as He builds up His people.

We need to learn more about praying strategically. What we have seen in eastern Europe in these past few years is a beautiful thing. However, this is a time when we need to be strategically praying against the forces of wickedness in the heavenly places, because the last thing we want to see is the church in Eastern Europe become like the church in Western Europe. Eastern Europe, until recent revolutions, has been a stronghold for persecution, but western Europe has been a stronghold for consumerism and apathy toward God. The church in eastern Europe is very alive in the midst of its needs, persecutions and pressures. In many churches that are opening up in Russia and the eastern bloc countries, there are long lines of hungry people waiting to come in to worship. Many of the churches in Western Europe are museums; it is a spiritual desert. We need to be praying now for the church in Eastern Europe, that God would preserve their spiritual fervor and that He would keep their hearts and continue to give life to them. We must intercede before the Lord, asking that they would not lose what He has given to them in the midst of the growing abundance the West will bring, as the materialism and the pornography pour in faster than we can take in Bibles. Tremendous battles are taking place that are centered in the realms of the heavenlies, not in the realm of time and space. That is why we need to learn to pray strategically.

There are other strong applications in the call for strategic prayer. When we are facing needs for workers in our churches such as teachers, counselors, leaders and servants, we tend to trust in our persuasiveness. We sometimes pressure people or we recruit volunteers. There are two other strategies in the Scriptures for raising up workers. One strategy is worship, which we see in Isaiah 6:1 and Acts 13:1-3. God raises up workers in an environment of worship. The other strategy is prayer. How did our Lord instruct us to seek workers? Jesus said, as He sent His disciples out into ministry:

> After this the Lord appointed seventy-two others and sent them on ahead of him, two by two, into every town and place where he himself was about to go. And he said to them, "The harvest is plentiful, but the laborers are few. Therefore pray earnestly to the Lord of the harvest to send out laborers into his harvest." (Luke 10:1-2)

We can actually participate with our sovereign Father in the fulfilling of His will and the building of His Kingdom through prayer! The real battles of our lives and ministries are fought and won in the realm of prayer.

BATTLES IN THE HEAVENLIES

There is a wonderful picture of this truth in the Old Testament. In the book of Exodus, Israel was in battle with the Amalekites. Joshua was leading the troops on the battlefield while Moses was on the mountain praying. When he would lift up his hands in prayer, the people of God would prevail. When his hands became tired and he stopped praying, the enemy prevailed.

> So Joshua did as Moses told him, and fought with Amalek, while Moses, Aaron, and Hur went up to the top of the hill. Whenever Moses held up his hand, Israel prevailed, and whenever he lowered his hand, Amalek prevailed. But Moses' hands grew weary, so they took a stone and put it under him, and he sat on it, while Aaron and Hur held up his hands, one on one side, and the other on the other side. So his hands were steady until the going down of the sun. And Joshua overwhelmed Amalek and his people with the sword. (Exodus 17:10-13)

This incident tells us something about prayer and also about the battles of our lives. Although this battle was physically fought in the valley before the mountain where Moses was praying, the real war was taking place in the realm of the heavenlies. This victory was won in the realm of prayer. The battles in our lives and the lives of those whom God has entrusted to us in ministry are not taking place in the physical/temporal realm; they are not against flesh and blood, but against the spiritual forces of wickedness in the heavenly places. Nothing we can do or say will make any difference in those battles. God has invited us to participate with Him in great power through prayer in the victories that are His in the realms of time and space, and in the heavenlies.

LISTENING IN PRAYER

> In these days he went out to the mountain to pray, and all night he continued in prayer to God. And when day came, he called his disciples and chose from them twelve, whom he named apostles: (Luke 6:12-13)

These two verses from Luke's large Gospel are so revealing about Jesus and His ministry. Jesus went up on the mountain and spent the entire night in prayer with His Father. Can you visualize this scene? Can you see Jesus praying all night? What do you see happening as He is praying? Do you think He lost His voice during this night from so many hours of talking? Of course not! Jesus knew something about prayer that we have a hard time learning. He knew that His Father had far more to say to Him than He had to say to His Father. He spent this time listening.

Jesus knew by the leading of the Holy Spirit that this was the Father's timing to focus His heart and ministry into a handful of men. There were hundreds of disciples who had been following Him, learning the truths of life in His Kingdom and responding to the teaching. Now the Son of God knew that it was the Father's timing to prepare a handful of men for that work of building the church. Thus, He went up on the mountain and listened to His Father. He was seeking His Father's mind, heart and direction. Who would God give Him for this ministry? While He was listening and praying, God was putting into Jesus' heart the very men He would give Him as apostles.

If Christ's example is a picture for us, then prayer is not primarily an opportunity to ask God to do things for us, but a time of communion in which He is glorified and in which He gives us His direction and strength for ministry. We need to learn to "listen" in prayer, to be sensitive as God speaks through His Word and His Spirit. It is in the intimacy of this "listen/respond" relationship that God builds His heart into us. We so often struggle with a lack of direction in our personal lives, our churches and in our ministries. Could this reflect a lack in our prayer lives? We have difficulty listening; we have difficulty discerning the voice of our shepherd in the midst of all the other voices that are coming at us continually. So much of our prayer lives is spent in taking to God the things we desire Him to do. Like Jesus, we must learn to listen.

DIRECTION IN MINISTRY

In Acts 2 we find recorded the Day of Pentecost in which the Holy Spirit came upon the church and gave them great power. The first chapter of Acts is just as important, as there we find the environment in which the Holy Spirit came.

> While staying with them he ordered them not to depart from Jerusalem, but to wait for the promise of the Father, which, he said, "you heard from me; for John baptized with water, but you will be baptized with the Holy Spirit not many days from now." (Acts 1:4-5)

Jesus had risen from the dead and had been with His disciples for forty days. As He prepared to return to His Father, Jesus instructed the disciples to wait for the Holy Spirit.

> They returned to Jerusalem from the mount called Olivet, which is near Jerusalem, a Sabbath day's journey away. And when they had entered, they went up to the upper room, where they were staying, Peter and John and James and Andrew, Philip and Thomas, Bartholomew and Matthew, James the son of Alphaeus and Simon the Zealot and Judas the son of James. All these with

one accord were devoting themselves to prayer, together with the women and Mary the mother of Jesus, and his brothers. (Acts 1:12-14)

There were about 120 people gathered in that room for a period of ten days. The first thing we see on the part of the disciples is sheer obedience. Jesus told them to go back to Jerusalem and wait. Since their Master had just been crucified, Jerusalem might not have been a very comfortable place for the followers of Jesus. They went back into the upper room and waited. They were all joined together in constant prayer in that upper room.

How long is long enough to pray? The disciples did not know it would be ten days before the Holy Spirit came. Jesus had said, "In a few days." But "a few days" with God can be many days to us! Have you ever had the powerful experience of being at an all-night prayer meeting or at a prayer retreat in which you pray over a number of days? How long is long enough to pray?

Would it not have been understandable if after five or six days in prayer one of the "real leaders" in that group stood up and said, "Now we have just been given a great commission from the Master. We've been commanded to go not only to Jerusalem, Judea and Samaria but also to the entire world with the message of the risen Christ. Who are the best speakers in the group? Why don't you gather here and decide who should be the primary ones to take the message? Who are the best organizers? Why don't you go over there and talk together about how we can most strategically and efficiently get the message out? Who are the ones to handle finances of the project? Who should let the people in the cities and towns know that the message is coming?" Wouldn't it have been understandable if they had divided up into committees? However, this was the emptying process before the filling process! All of their plans, their goals, their hopes and their

Adequate!

dreams were being removed by the Holy Spirit. In prayer God was uniting their hearts into His and into one another's, giving them one common vision and purpose. The Spirit then came and filled the church of the Lord Jesus, as God's people were "joined together constantly in prayer." God gave direction for the ministry they would share.

AN ANSWER BIGGER THAN WE WERE SEEKING

A few years ago we were facing a great financial crisis at our home church. We had a large payment of over $25,000 that was due on a particular date. Because we have a commitment in our church not to pressure or manipulate our people financially, we sent out a letter making them aware of the need and asking them to pray. The payment was due on a Monday. The Sunday morning before the bill was due, it was announced from the pulpit that there would be a brief board meeting after the morning service. When we met with the elders and deacons, we found that for this great need, only a very small amount of money had been contributed. "What do we do now?" the leaders asked. Some of the men had suggestions, and then by the grace of God one of them said, "There is nothing we can do. We need to pray." His direction was quickly affirmed. We all decided we would take our families home and come directly back to the church to spend the afternoon in prayer.

When we returned, we gathered in a circle, shared a few thoughts, quoted a few verses, then got down on our knees and began to pray. After just a few moments of thanking the Lord for His presence among us and bringing this need to Him, the prayers of the men began to change. Rather than the primary desire for this bill to be paid and our need to be met, the men began to seek God's glory first in the situation. I remember many men praying, "God, whatever you choose to do, however you choose to do it, more than anything else we want you to be glorified." Then without a suggestion and without our talking about it, something most amazing happened. The men began to confess their sins to the Lord and to one another. One after another, we confessed our sins.

After a long period of prayer, we sat in the circle of chairs once again and looked at each other. We were no closer to an answer than we were before we began to pray. "What do we do now?" some of the men asked. "Why don't we just keep praying and share with the people at the evening service what God did this afternoon?" others suggested. After the service something miraculous took place, but not nearly as miraculous as what had happened that afternoon. People began to come up to the pastors, to the men on the board, and to the financial officers and hand them checks. Before the evening was over, we had far more money than was needed to pay that debt. We will never forget that day, and how God met us and provided for us as we prayed.

God gives direction for ministry in the environment of prayer. We tend to become consumed with what we are doing and how we must do it. We so often try to "make things happen" by means of our resources. In prayer God gives direction for ministry. We saw that with His Son and with the First Century Christians. We, too, must learn to seek the Lord in prayer and to listen for the direction He gives.

We see this same encouragement in Acts 13. What a model for us is the church in Antioch! They possessed a great heart for missions and were free to send out their best people. They had also learned to listen in prayer and to receive direction for ministry.

Now there were in the church at Antioch prophets and teachers, Barnabas, Simeon who was called Niger, Lucius of Cyrene, Manaen a member of the court of Herod the tetrarch, and Saul. While they were worshiping the Lord and fasting, the Holy Spirit

171

said, "Set apart for me Barnabas and Saul for the work to which I have called them." Then after fasting and praying they laid their hands on them and sent them off. (Acts 13:1-3)

What a picture! Would they have thought of sending out Saul and Barnabas? Saul was still untested and many mistrusted him. Would this have been their strategy? As they came before the Lord in worship and fasting, in the environment of prayer, God spoke to them and gave direction for their ministry.

A lack of direction in ministry might reflect a lack in our prayer lives. When we are sufficient for what God has set before us, we have no need to pray. As we saw in the church at Jerusalem, when we come to the end of ourselves and seek the Lord in prayer, there is an emptying process and then God's filling process. As He gives us life, power and direction, God does something wonderful, miraculous and eternal as we pray. He knits our hearts together in prayer, not only with one another's but also with His. As we commune with Him, God opens our eyes to see what He sees and moves us to walk with Him in what He is doing.

Pray, Then, in This Way

As Luke records it, the Lord's Prayer was given when the disciples asked Jesus to teach them to pray after He Himself had spent time in prayer alone. Matthew also recorded this prayer near the beginning of Jesus' ministry with His disciples.

Pray then like this: "Our Father in heaven, hallowed be your name. Your kingdom come, your will be done, on earth as it is in heaven." (Matthew 6:9-10)

I can imagine the scene as Jesus is teaching, and I can see the eyes of the disciples opening wider and wider in awe and wonder. Our Lord is introducing a new Kingdom and a new relationship with God. When you pray, you say "Our Father!"

Abraham, who was God's friend never referred to Him as Father. Moses, who spoke with God face to face never addressed God as Father. David, the man after God's own heart never called Him Father. Jesus is introducing a new covenant that will be sealed in His own blood. Those who come to God through Him will now know the Creator of the ends of the earth, the sovereign God who rules with power, the God of glory so brilliant that we would die if we saw Him, the holy One who is high and lifted up, as *Abba Father!* Like a child crawling into her father's lap, confident she will be accepted, affirmed and loved, we run to God as His children, eager for this relationship of intimacy, life and joy.

In prayer we are taught to recognize who God is and to bring our reverence and worship before Him. Christ taught us also to express our desire for the reality of His Kingdom in our midst and that God's will be done here, in our lives and ministries, just as it is done in heaven. Prayer is the relationship in which we become the vessels through which God's will can be freely fulfilled in this world.

> Give us this day our daily bread, and forgive us our debts, as we also have forgiven our debtors. (Matthew 6:11-12)

Christ taught us to ask God for the material things we need just for today, and to ask forgiveness for our sins as we are also expressing that forgiving love in our relationships with one another. Jesus continued in His prayer by asking that as God leads our steps this day, He might not lead us into temptation but bring deliverance from the evil one.

> And lead us not into temptation, but deliver us from evil. (Matthew 6:13)

Christ began His prayer with reverence for who God is, and He closed His prayer with praise for what belongs to Him: the

173

Kingdom He is building out of His own heart, the power by which He fulfills His work, and the glory which belongs to Him alone. As Jesus began to talk to His disciples again, He came back to the part of the prayer concerning forgiveness. Our relationship with God is "mirrored" in our relationships with one another. Again it is clear that if we do not reflect back to God His own heart during our times of communion with Him, our prayer is meaningless.

> If you forgive others their trespasses, your heavenly Father will also forgive you, but if you do not forgive others their trespasses, neither will your Father forgive your trespasses. (Matthew 6:14-15)

WHY DO WE STRUGGLE?

So many of us struggle with our prayer lives. Almost everyone I know desires a prayer life characterized by deeper intimacy and power. As we share with one another why we battle in this area, we might talk about our priorities and the fact that we are not disciplined enough for a consistent prayer time. We tend to become consumed in what we are doing and do not take the time to develop a communion relationship with God. Others of us say, "I have never really been taught to pray. I'm not sure how to go about it. What do you say to God? I get together a list of things I want God to do for me, and I thank Him for what He's already done. Then I run out of things to say."

I think there is another battle going on here—one that is taking place both in the heavenlies and in our hearts. Satan, the accuser of the brethren (Revelation 12:10), is causing us to see ourselves through his eyes, rather than the eyes of God. He is slandering us before the Lord and before our own hearts, seeking to steal away from us a freedom and confidence in our relationship with God.

Perhaps you have noticed that when you have had opportunities and are just about to begin ministry—serving, teaching, counseling or sharing your faith—you are overwhelmed with a sense of inadequacy. There are good reasons why we feel inadequate: We *are* inadequate! We are inadequate in ourselves, but God makes us adequate as servants of a new covenant. As we approach those ministry opportunities, our enemy might say to us, "You know, your ministry in your own family isn't really what it ought to be. You are not giving yourself to your wife the way you should or responding to your husband the way you should. You are not teaching your children the way you should or spending as much time with them as you ought. What makes you think that God is going to use you in this new ministry opportunity when you are not even taking care of your present responsibilities? Don't you think that you ought to get your ministry right in your own family and then let God use you over here?" We listen to his voice, which seems to make so much sense to either a hurting heart or a fleshly mind, and we withdraw.

There may have been other times when you have been praying, and after a brief time, you feel as if your prayers are just "bouncing off the ceiling." You sense that you are not touching God's heart, so you give up. It is at times like this, when we desire to commune with God and to pray with power, that Satan will remind us of every sin we have committed, every failure of our lives, every weakness of our hearts, and all our inconsistencies. He will even quote the Scriptures to us and say, "You remember how the Bible tells us that the prayer of a righteous man is powerful and effective (James 5:16)? That is true. But you do not really believe that you are a righteous person, do you? Surely you remember a few days ago, driving down the street and seeing that beautiful young girl and the lustful thoughts and feelings with which you responded? Would a righteous man respond like that? Of course not! You should make yourself more righteous and then come back to God; then maybe He'll listen to you when you pray."

Satan may seek to manipulate a woman in the same way by saying, "Remember the other day when you walked into that woman's house and saw all the beautiful things in her home that for many years you have dreamed of having? Do you remember how jealousy and envy filled your heart? Now if you were really a righteous woman, wouldn't your first response have been to thank God for the way He has blessed this woman? You are only kidding yourself if you think you are a spiritual woman. You had better work a bit more and make yourself more righteous, then God will hear you when you pray."

The deception in what Satan is bringing to us is so powerfully destructive. Some of the things he is talking to us about might very well have to be dealt with, but they do not mean what he says they mean. The central issue is that he is causing us to see ourselves in terms of our weaknesses, our sins, our failures, our past, and our feelings. He is manipulating us to see ourselves through his eyes rather than the eyes of God. He is stealing away from us boldness in ministry and power in prayer. This is why we battle with our prayer lives. This is a battle taking place in the realms of the heavenlies, against the powers of this dark world. Satan is seeking to steal away from us a freedom in God's presence. He will continually remind us that God is a holy and righteous God and ask what right we have to come into His presence.

We do have a right to come into God's presence. That right is not won by our spiritual performances; it is purchased by the blood of Christ. The writer to the Hebrews said this:

> Let us then with confidence draw near to the throne of grace, that we may receive mercy and find grace to help in time of need. (Hebrews 4:16)

The apostle Paul wrote to the church at Ephesus, referring to our great high priest, the Lord Jesus,

> in whom we have boldness and access with confidence through our faith in him. (Ephesians 3:12)

We have bold and confident access to the throne of God and great freedom in His presence! We do not come confidently because we have performed well recently or because we have been having our devotions consistently or because we have not missed too many church services lately or because we have been giving our money the way we should. No, we come confidently because we are clothed in the righteousness of Jesus and therefore have access to the throne of grace. Satan is manipulating us, seeking to steal away that prayer relationship of intimacy and of power. He knows that spiritual battles are won in the environment of prayer, and he is trying to get us out of the battle and onto the sidelines, consuming all our spiritual resources wondering about the state of our relationship with God and whether we are spiritual enough to pray. God has called us, even as creatures of dust, to commune with Him and to participate with Him through prayer in the fulfillment of His will. We cannot allow Satan to cheaply steal away from us that which God has given us at such a great price. We must take hold of this gift that God has provided in the death of His Son and walk in all the boldness, freedom, and confidence right into His presence and pray!

QUESTIONS FOR COMMUNICATION AND APPLICATION

1. What are the characteristics of your prayer life, and what do they say about your relationship with the Lord?

    A. How much time do you spend in prayer?

    B. Do you find yourself talking more than you listen?

    C. Do you ask God to teach you how to see people and how He might use you as part of His process in their lives?

    D. Do you try to badger God into changing His mind rather than ask Him to change you?

2. How might your times of prayer become more of a communion relationship with the Lord and a time that glorifies Him?

3. In your times of prayer, have you seen God building His heart and mind into you and making you like Himself? In what areas have you seen this transformation take place?

As each has received a gift, use it to serve one another, as good stewards of God's varied grace: whoever speaks, as one who speaks oracles of God; whoever serves, as one who serves by the strength that God supplies—in order that in everything God may be glorified through Jesus Christ. To him belong glory and dominion forever and ever. Amen.

1 Peter 4:10-11

6
A Community of Servants

In order for us to be ministers together of God's new covenant, we must know the nature of the life He has given us in His Son and how to walk with one another. He has made us a community of His people to serve one another with His very life! There is only one role in God's Kingdom: the role of a servant. There is one Lord; all the rest of us are servants of one another with varying responsibilities in each other's lives. Christ taught His disciples that if their ministry to one another was to be effective, they needed to learn to look at one another through the eyes of a servant, for in an environment of serving the Word of God comes alive in a fruitful ministry to one another.

AMONG ONE ANOTHER AS THOSE WHO SERVE

We love to read about the twelve men Christ personally chose for the building of His Church. We look at their lives and say, "If God could use them, He can surely use me!" Often the disciples lived on the level of little children on a school playground, caught up in the games that would separate the winners from the losers.

> They came to Capernaum. And when he was in the house he asked them, "What were you discussing on the way?" But they kept silent, for on the way they had argued with one another about who was the greatest. (Mark 9:33-34)

One day as Jesus and His band of followers were on their way from one town to another, we find His disciples arguing with each other about which one was the greatest, competing with each other for the highest position on the basis of their knowledge, accomplishments, personality or gifts.

> He sat down and called the twelve. And he said to them, "If anyone would be first, he must be last of all and servant of all." (Mark 9:35)

Christ would not permit this competitive spirit among His followers. He taught them that in His Kingdom, greatness is discerned in a completely new way. In this world we look for the one who is the first and the best, the one with the most abilities and resources. God looks for the one who is willing to be last and the least.

> He took a child and put him in the midst of them, and taking him in his arms, he said to them, "Whoever receives one such child in my name receives me, and whoever receives me, receives not me but him who sent me." (Mark 9:36-37)

Why would the Lord pick up a child to teach His disciples the lesson they must learn? In that society the value of a child increased with its ability to contribute to either the household or the family business. Until that time, the child was often a liability to its parents in the midst of great financial pressures. However, as the child's knowledge and accomplishments grew, so he grew in value. Christ is teaching His disciples a concept of intrinsic value and worth. This child is to be greatly valued because of who he is in God's eyes, precious because of His workmanship and

His image. This child's value had nothing to do with what he could produce or how he could contribute, and everything to do with who he is in God's sight. Only when we understand our basic value, worth, acceptance, and approval before our Father in heaven can we be free from the fluctuating value system in this world which depends on our production and performance. Only then are we free to serve one another from that full position of strength with God.

> A dispute also arose among them, as to which of them was to be regarded as the greatest. (Luke 22:24)

There were other times also when Jesus' disciples competed with each other for the greatest position.

> He said to them, "The kings of the Gentiles exercise lordship over them, and those in authority over them are called benefactors." (Luke 22:25)

Christ wanted His disciples to know that we pursue life one way in this world but another way in His Kingdom. In this world we look at one another with the desire to elevate ourselves, to place ourselves above others and to "lord it over them." We love to look at people from an elevated position. We enjoy handing down to them what they need from us, whether it is things or help or encouragement.

> But not so with you. Rather, let the greatest among you become as the youngest, and the leader as one who serves. (Luke 22:26)

The manipulations of one another in order to enhance ourselves is part of our old life in this system. In His everlasting Kingdom, those who desire to be leaders take the position of servants in their relationships with one another. Greatness in the Kingdom of God is not measured by what we know, by what we have accomplished, or by where we have been. It is seen only in our willingness to take the lowest place and to lay down our lives for one another.

> Who is the greater, one who reclines at table or one who serves? Is it not the one who reclines at table? But I am among you as the one who serves. (Luke 22:27)

In this world it is easy to recognize the great ones, for they are those with positions in which others serve them. Jesus Christ, the Lord of the universe, came into the world not as one to be served but as one who gave Himself up for others. The Creator came to serve His creatures. If the One with all the authority, all the high position, all the right to be served came with the heart of a servant, how much more must our relationships with one another reflect His heart!

WASH ONE ANOTHER'S FEET

When we ask God to make Christ's attitude our own and we have the resources of the Holy Spirit with which to live out that commitment love in our relationships with one another, then we have the personal environment in which ministry can be communicated effectively.

The last night Jesus spent with them before going to the cross, He demonstrated the purpose of His coming in a beautiful way.

> During supper, when the devil had already put it into the heart of Judas Iscariot, Simon's son, to betray him, Jesus, knowing that the Father had given all things into his hands, and that he had come from God and was going back to God, rose from supper. He laid aside his outer garments, and taking a towel, tied it around his waist. (John 13:2-4)

Christ was physically picturing what Paul would later describe to the Philippians (2:1-11). Rather than grasping on to His equality with God, He took up the form of a servant. Now, before the Last Supper, He laid aside the garments which rightfully belonged to Him and picked up the towel and basin that belonged to the servant.

> Then he poured water into a basin and began to wash the disciples' feet and to wipe them with the towel that was wrapped around him. He came to Simon Peter, who said to him, "Lord, do you wash my feet?" (John 13:5-6)

Using the water, the basin and the towel, Christ began to wash the feet of His disciples. This particular task was usually performed for guests by the lowest servant in the house. Peter could not accept the fact that Jesus Christ, the exalted Lord and Holy God, was about to wash his feet.

> Jesus answered him, "What I am doing you do not understand now, but afterward you will understand." Peter said to him, "You shall never wash my feet." Jesus answered him, "If I do not wash you, you have no share with me." (John 13:7-8)

Christ assured Peter that there was more taking place here than he was able to perceive, but Peter continued to react against Him and His humility. Jesus rebuked him, telling him that only those whom He cleanses can share His life.

> Simon Peter said to him, "Lord, not my feet only but also my hands and my head!" Jesus said to him, "The one who has bathed does not need to wash, except for his feet, but is completely clean. And you are clean, but not every one of you." For he knew who was to betray him; that was why he said, "Not all of you are clean." (John 13:9-11)

Peter then asked Christ to wash him totally, but Christ assured him that one who has already been cleansed needs only his feet washed to be completely clean again. In John 15:3 Christ told His disciples, "You are already clean because of the word I have spoken to you." During the years He had been ministering to His disciples, Jesus had been cleansing them with His Word day by day, in His teaching, His rebukes, His encouragement, and His example. Now only their feet needed to be washed in order for them to be completely clean again.

> When he had washed their feet and put on his outer garments and resumed his place, he said to them, "Do you understand what I have done to you?" (John 13:12)

We can visualize the scene as Jesus is washing His disciples' feet. One by one He kneels before them in amazing humility, gently washes their feet and dries them with the towel—all around the room, each of the disciples' feet washed by the same hands that created the stars and placed the planets in their orbits. After He finished, He said, "Do you understand what I have done to you?" Jesus has just washed the feet of the man who in a few moments will betray Him to death. What a display of God's power within us that enables us to serve one another, and even our enemies!

> You call me Teacher and Lord, and you are right, for so I am. If I then, your Lord and Teacher, have washed your feet, you also ought to wash one another's feet. For I have given you an example, that you also should do just as I have done to you. (John 13:13-15)

If the One who holds the highest place is willing to take the lowest position, do the most humbling thing even for His greatest enemy, how can we do less and expect to have a ministry which expresses the fruit of God's heart? Christ wanted His disciples to look at one another and ask, "How can I give myself up for you so that you can develop and grow? How can I submit to you, elevate you above myself and serve you, even if that means taking the lowest place possible and doing the thing everyone else avoids?" Ministry flows only from that kind of heart.

> Truly, truly, I say to you, a servant is not greater than his master, nor is a messenger greater than the one who sent him. If you know these things, blessed are you if you do them. (John 13:16-17)

As those who are sent, we are servants who bring the heart of God to one another, rather than seeking to build our own kingdom. We do not have any authority apart from what God gives to us. We are servants who are filled with resources from God given to build up one another. Christ's example is clear in demonstrating how to do that. When we see needs, we give ourselves up to meet them in a brother's or sister's life, knowing that on some level this will mean laying down our lives. It is important to remember that Jesus said that those blessed of God are not the ones who know these beautiful and powerful truths, for in God's sight possession of knowledge alone is of very little value. The ones who receive the approval of the living God are the ones who appropriate these attitudes into the fabric of a Christlike lifestyle.

ACCEPT ONE ANOTHER

In the kingdom of this world we develop relationships of convenience. We are drawn to people who can contribute to what we need, what builds us up and to our sense of well being. We are often repulsed by those we consider weak. God desires to teach us to respond to one another in a new way.

> We who are strong have an obligation to bear with the failings of the weak, and not to please ourselves. (Romans 15:1)

The exhortation to "not just please ourselves" runs completely against the grain of our fleshly desires. No one would ever choose to live that way if left to himself; only God can teach us to focus on the good of another person and to give ourselves to build him up.

> Let each of us please his neighbor for his good, to build him up. For Christ did not please himself, but as it is written, "The reproaches of those who reproached you fell on me." (Romans 15:2-3)

Again, Christ is our supreme example of One who did not live for the purpose of pleasing Himself. He came in order to bear in His body the pain which belonged to us and to absorb the hatred of humankind toward the Father. He did all this for our good and for the purpose of building us up.

> Whatever was written in former days was written for our instruction, that through endurance and through the encouragement of the Scriptures we might have hope. (Romans 15:4)

In the Scriptures God has given us examples to teach us how to walk with Him. He is continually demonstrating His patience with us and building endurance into us so that we do not yield ourselves up to the ways of this world, but walk with God in His ways of building up one another. God does not allow us to die in our failures; He has continually given us hope through the encouragement of His Word.

> May the God of endurance and encouragement grant you to live in such harmony with one another, in accord with Christ Jesus, that together you may with one voice glorify the God and Father of our Lord Jesus Christ. (Romans 15:5-6)

God perseveres in His patient love toward us and fills our heart with hope, and He desires us to have the same attitude with one another. The attitude toward us which Christ demonstrated on the cross is our example for relationships with each other.

This mind-set, beginning with the heart of a servant flowing into the ability to persevere with one another and to sustain each other's heart with hope, overflows in unity, worship and the glory of God.

Welcome one another as Christ has welcomed you, for the glory of God. (Romans 15:7)

When we were so weak that we could not demonstrate godliness in any way and were covered with all the ugliness and dirt of sin, Christ did not leave us to ourselves for eternal judgment. Because of His everlasting love and the glory of His Father, Christ accepted us into Himself at the cost of His own life. Now we have that pattern for our relationships with one another. We do not walk out of each other's lives at the first point of difficulty in our relationship; we do not give up at the first sign of failure; we are not repulsed at the first evidence of weakness and sin. God has taught us to persevere with one another as He has done with us and to encourage each other with the Scriptures in order that we might have hope. We now give one another reasons to keep going on with God rather than walk away and let another person slowly die all alone.

You have not delivered me into the hand of the enemy; you have set my feet in a broad place. (Psalm 31:8)

David reveals much of the character of God in this beautiful psalm. He understands how God sees him and how He works in his life. David tells us that God does not give up on him and allow his enemies to control him; instead, God gives him expanded places in which to walk. In this world apart from God, we live tightly squeezed into little places and become little people in the process. We have the continual pressure of having to perform in exactly the accepted way at every point in life. It is not that way with God. With Him we have room to be real people, to be able to live in the expanded places He gives to us so that we can walk with freedom. There is no pressured performance, no tightly squeezed lifestyle. In our relationship with God we have large places in which to grow and even to fail without fear of rejection.

That is the way God desires us to live with each other. The Body of Christ is not to be made up of little people living in tight little places, pressured every moment to perform in a narrowly accepted way. We do the same thing with one another that God does with us; we give one another room. Only in this way can we live with the confidence that we will always be accepted, and the knowledge that our brothers and sisters will always persevere with us and give us the hope that comes from God's Word.

Bear One Another's Burdens

There is a great concern within the Body of Christ for one another's spiritual growth and for the battle in which we strive together against the world, the flesh and the devil. When one member of the Body suffers the pain of failure or hurt in any way, that affects every other member as well, because our lives are so intimately intertwined with each other's.

> If one member suffers, all suffer together; if one member is honored, all rejoice together. Now you are the body of Christ and individually members of it. (1 Corinthians 12:26-27)

Paul wrote to the Corinthians to express his identification with them in their struggle with sin and his deep concern for their spiritual welfare.

> Who is weak, and I am not weak? Who is made to fall, and I am not indignant? (2 Corinthians 11:29)

It is with this same level of concern and an attitude of mutual responsibility that Paul spoke to the Galatian Christians.

> Brothers, if anyone is caught in any transgression, you who are spiritual should restore him in a spirit of gentleness. Keep watch on yourself, lest you too be tempted. (Galatians 6:1)

When we see brothers or sisters struggling with any area of sin, we have a responsibility to confront them in love and seek to restore them in the faith. We must declare what is sin for their sake and encourage them to be obedient to God's Word in that area of their lives. This ministry is carried out in a spirit of meekness and gentleness and with deep and genuine compassion, never with an attitude of spiritual pride. We are always conscious of our own weakness, and undoubtedly, we will need that very same ministry on their part to us at another time.

> Bear one another's burdens, and so fulfill the law of Christ. For if anyone thinks he is something, when he is nothing, he deceives himself. (Galatians 6:2-3)

The weight of sin is so heavy and its results so devastating in our lives that no one is able to carry the burden alone. We often have blind spots that keep us from being aware of our own sin, though others watching us may see it clearly. If we see brothers or sisters caught in sin, we must never turn our back and fail to become involved. We are involved with them because we are members not only of Christ but also of one another. We have a responsibility before God to bear with them during times of weakness. This is the depth of love which the law of Christ is all about—loving and caring for one another to the degree that He has loved us. When we fail to confront other members of the Body of Christ about sin in their lives, it reveals pride in our heart. It feels much better to stand aloof from and to look down in judgment on one who has failed. That aloofness helps to solidify a false understanding of ourselves as better or more spiritual than our hurt brother or sister. This attitude reveals how deceived we are about ourselves and about the nature of our lives together as brothers and sisters.

> If your brother sins against you, go and tell him his fault, between you and him alone. If he listens to you, you have gained your brother. But if he does not listen, take one or two others along with you, that every charge may be established by the evidence of two or three witnesses. If he refuses to listen to them, tell it to the church. And if he refuses to listen even to the church, let him be to you as a Gentile and a tax collector. (Matthew 18:15-17)

When we deal with a brother or sister who has sinned, we must follow God's pattern of restoration.

First is a personal confrontation with the desire to win his or her response to the Lord, and second is a ministry of the Scriptures with another brother or sister present. If there is still no response to the Word of God, we must tell the entire church, which must continually call them to repentance and restoration. If they still refuse to repent, we must respond to them as if they are unbelievers, as the church of Christ must be kept pure because we serve a righteous God. This degree of discipline within the Body of Christ is always aimed at complete restoration of the individual member as well as the continual purity of the Bride of Christ.

BEAR WITH ONE ANOTHER

There is a reason why we are able to have deep, healing love relationships in our churches. That reason is not found in the fact that we do not hurt one another, for we are made out of dust, and we still hurt one another from time to time. Sometimes our words and actions are far less than God desires, and the pain which results in each other's lives is very real. Our relationships of depth and intimacy grow out of the way in which we respond when someone hurts us.

> Put on then, as God's chosen ones, holy and beloved, compassion, kindness, humility, meekness, and patience, bearing with one another and, if one has a complaint against another, forgiving each other; as the Lord has forgiven you, so you also must forgive. (Colossians 3:12-13)

How we respond to one another is always a result of who we are in Christ. God tells us that we are His chosen ones, made pure by the blood of Christ and loved with His everlasting love. He exhorts us now to bring the same transforming love of a new creation to one another. With this compassionate kindness and humble, gentle patience, we are able to bear with others when they hurt us rather than striking back at them. We are able to forgive them rather than being consumed by hatred and bitterness. Christ's love is our example as well as the power which enables us to respond in this way.

> Above all these put on love, which binds everything together in perfect harmony. And let the peace of Christ rule in your hearts, to which indeed you were called in one body. And be thankful. (Colossians 3:14-15)

This love characterized by commitment and giving cements our relationships with one another and enables us to endure through any degree of hurt without walking away. When Christ's peace rules our hearts, there are no fragile relationships in our churches. We are able to go through anything with each other, and as we respond with God's healing love, come through that time stronger together than we have ever been before. The perfect bond of Christ's love applied in times of pain unites our hearts in a way that can never be broken. His love never fails.

We have been conditioned in this world to strike back when someone hurts us. We do this with our actions and with our words in order to protect ourselves from further pain. Christ gave us another example; He placed Himself in a position to be hurt in order that we might be healed. He returned forgiveness for pain and blessings rather than more insults. He bore our sins in His body on the cross that we might live. That depth of forgiving love to which we are called becomes the norm in the Body of Christ, even in a system where the people around us are destroying one another with the pain that overflows in their relationships.

> Finally, all of you, have unity of mind, sympathy, brotherly love, a tender heart, and a humble mind. Do not repay evil for evil or reviling for reviling, but on the contrary, bless, for to this you were called, that you may obtain a blessing. (1 Peter 3:8-9)

CONFESS YOUR SINS TO ONE ANOTHER

We often tend to live isolated lives, hiding in the darkness from one another. Even after we become believers in Christ and members of His Body, we sometimes follow our old pattern of closing ourselves off from each other, even from those on whom we depend for our very lives!

Churches are not made up of perfect people. We are all in the process of being healed, of learning to walk with God and with one another. Not one of us has yet arrived at a point of perfection. All of us are dust, with many weaknesses where we need each other's strength. Yet we may close ourselves off from each other because we fear the rejection of those around us.

James wrote to teach about a major aspect of the healing process that is shared among one another as believers:

Is anyone among you sick? Let him call for the elders of the church, and let them pray over him, anointing him with oil in the name of the Lord. And the prayer of faith will save the one who is sick, and the Lord will raise him up. And if he has committed sins, he will be forgiven. (James 5:14-15)

God gives strong, specific direction for dealing with sickness and with spiritual weakness. The one who is sick, weakened in the battles with the evil one, must call for the elders. Prayers are to be offered on his behalf, sins are to be confessed, and he is to be anointed with oil in Christ's name. God gives us hope that this is part of His healing process in our lives—not just physical healing, but spiritual healing as well.

Confess your sins to one another and pray for one another, that you may be healed. The prayer of a righteous person has great power as it is working. (James 5:16)

God is bringing us to the place where we confess our sins to one another. Unconfessed sin can block God's healing power in our lives, and we desperately need each other's prayers when we are physically, emotionally or spiritually sick. There is great power in the prayers of righteous men and women. The relationship between unconfessed sin and physical sickness was clear in David's life:

When I kept silent, my bones wasted away through my groaning all day long. For day and night your hand was heavy upon me; my strength was dried up as by the heat of summer. *Selah* I acknowledged my sin to you, and I did not cover my iniquity; I said, "I will confess my transgressions to the LORD," and you forgave the iniquity of my sin. *Selah* (Psalm 32:3-5)

God desires us to live in "confessional relationships" with Himself and with one another. The willingness to reveal our sins is now the nature of our walk with God and with one another.

Adequate!

Just as we know that God accepts us totally in His Son, we need to have confidence in our acceptance of one another. Confession of sin is an important characteristic of the person who walks in the light. Our spiritual, emotional and physical health are dependent on our freedom to confess our sins to God and to one another. We must continually exercise the ministry of God's Word together in this area.

> If we confess our sins, he is faithful and just to forgive us our sins and to cleanse us from all unrighteousness. (1 John 1:9)

SHARE WITH ONE ANOTHER

The New Testament Church was filled with the power of God. The ministry of the apostles was marked by signs and wonders; those who participated and those who watched were in awe of the living God.

> Awe came upon every soul, and many wonders and signs were being done through the apostles. (Acts 2:43)

Inseparably linked to the power in their presence was their attitude toward one another and the way they handled the material things God had given them.

> All who believed were together and had all things in common. And they were selling their possessions and belongings and distributing the proceeds to all, as any had need. (Acts 2:44-45)

There is a direct relationship in any church between the power of God expressed there, and their attitude toward their finances in relationship to one another. When we see the New Testament Church flourishing, we also see a very real commitment to share material things with each other. When they became aware of needs in one another's lives, their immediate response was to sell property or possessions to meet those needs.

The full number of those who believed were of one heart and soul, and no one said that any of the things that belonged to him was his own, but they had everything in common. And with great power the apostles were giving their testimony to the resurrection of the Lord Jesus, and great grace was upon them all. There was not a needy person among them, for as many as were owners of lands or houses sold them and brought the proceeds of what was sold and laid it at the apostles' feet, and it was distributed to each as any had need. (Acts 4:32-35)

The relationship is clear between the attitude they had toward their possessions and the power of God displayed in their midst. They clearly saw one another as more valuable than the things they possessed and freely claimed that nothing belonging to them was their own. The result was that God's grace was abundant on them all.

We live in a world that loves and worships things. God wants to teach us to worship Him alone and to love His people. Our roots are so deep in this materialistic realm that often even after coming to Christ, our lives are more characterized by a love for things than a commitment to people. The New Testament Church was willing to give up their things for one another, and they became abundant in grace. In our churches because we are abundant in things while many have great needs, this has perhaps cost us a great measure of God's grace. Have we chosen to become abundant in things rather than in grace? Surely God desires to have us possess the attitude of the New Testament believers, even if that means possessing fewer things.

TEACHING AND ADMONISHING ONE ANOTHER

The New Testament Church was filled with the ministry of God's Word. This ministry came not from only a few specially trained members, but from every member of the Body of Christ. God has designed the church to be characterized by a mutual ministry of His Word.

> Let the word of Christ dwell in you richly, teaching and admonishing one another in all wisdom, singing psalms and hymns and spiritual songs, with thankfulness in your hearts to God. And whatever you do, in word or deed, do everything in the name of the Lord Jesus, giving thanks to God the Father through him. (Colossians 3:16-17)

We are exhorted by the apostle Paul to allow the Word of God to live deeply and freely within us, and with the wisdom the Word gives, to have a ministry of the Scriptures in each other's lives. Of great significance is the ministry Paul describes—teaching and admonishing one another. Each member has the responsibility of giving the instruction from the Scriptures that leads to a godly life, and the confrontational encouragement that redirects another's behavior. This is a deep ministry that includes the spoken word as well as the music of the Scriptures which stimulates praise and thanksgiving.

> Do not get drunk with wine, for that is debauchery, but be filled with the Spirit, addressing one another in psalms and hymns and spiritual songs, singing and making melody to the Lord with all your heart, giving thanks always and for everything to God the Father in the name of our Lord Jesus Christ, (Ephesians 5:18-20)

Paul is teaching us as a church how to be filled with the Holy Spirit, a part of which is the mutual ministry of the Scriptures. This sharing of God's Word among one another develops an atmosphere in which genuine worship takes place.

As Paul encouraged the church at Rome to function as a Body of Believers, he began with the instruction to present their own bodies to God.

> I appeal to you therefore, brothers, by the mercies of God, to present your bodies as a living sacrifice, holy and acceptable to God, which is your spiritual worship. (Romans 12:1)

True worship is seeing God as worthy of all our lives, and then presenting all that we are and have as vessels to be used in the ministry of His life in this world. When we come together as a church, true worship takes place as we encourage one another with the Scriptures and present ourselves together to God as a living sacrifice. The Body of Christ is the environment where this happens! As Paul continues in this passage, he talks of serving one another as God has gifted us. Surely we cannot present our bodies to God without presenting ourselves within the Body of Christ and using our gifts for service and ministry.

As Paul wrote to the Ephesians, he described the growth process which builds toward a mature church.

> He gave the apostles, the prophets, the evangelists, the pastors and teachers, to equip the saints for the work of ministry, for building up the body of Christ, until we all attain to the unity of the faith and of the knowledge of the Son of God, to mature manhood, to the measure of the stature of the fullness of Christ, (Ephesians 4:11-13)

God has given mature leadership to churches to equip us for the work of the ministry. These leaders are given primarily to the ministry of the Word in the process which results in the building up of the Body of Christ. That equipping continues and the ministry is shared among the saints until there is genuine unity among the believers, a deep relationship with Christ characterized by full understanding, and a maturity that exhibits the fullness of Christ in their lives together,

> so that we may no longer be children, tossed to and fro by the waves and carried about by every wind of doctrine, by human

cunning, by craftiness in deceitful schemes. Rather, speaking the truth in love, we are to grow up in every way into him who is the head, into Christ, from whom the whole body, joined and held together by every joint with which it is equipped, when each part is working properly, makes the body grow so that it builds itself up in love. (Ephesians 4:14-16)

As the church walks together in this process, we grow up with one another in every aspect of the Christian life. We are characterized by stability, the ability to discern truth from error, and the love which we uniquely share in this world. This growth is a result of our holding fast together to the Head of the church, who is Christ, and contributing to one another the ministry which God has equipped us to bring to each other. What stimulates this process is speaking the truth in love to one another. Only in Christ can we tell each other the truth about Him, about ourselves and about one another. The Church of the Lord Jesus is the only environment in which we are secure enough to handle truth! The mutual ministry of the Word of God among the members of the Body of Christ provides the environment for this growth to maturity and characterizes a church in which God is alive in their midst.

LOVE ONE ANOTHER

A new commandment I give to you, that you love one another: just as I have loved you, you also are to love one another. By this all people will know that you are my disciples, if you have love for one another. (John 13:34-35)

God had summarized the Law as "Love the Lord your God with all your heart, and with all your soul, and with all your mind, and your neighbor as yourself" (Luke 10:27). Jesus was teaching His disciples that to love their neighbor as they loved themselves was not enough; to express God's love demanded that they love one another more than they loved their own lives. That is the way Christ loved us. When the world sees us exhibiting that self-sacrificing love in our relationships with one another, they will know the genuineness of our faith in Christ.

> Beloved, let us love one another, for love is from God, and whoever loves has been born of God and knows God. Anyone who does not love does not know God, because God is love. (1 John 4:7-8)

John, the great apostle who learned to love as he was loved by Christ, calls those to whom he is writing to express the reality of their relationship with Christ in the way in which they love one another. If we have received God's life, we have also received His nature, which is love.

> In this the love of God was made manifest among us, that God sent his only Son into the world, so that we might live through him. In this is love, not that we have loved God but that he loved us and sent his Son to be the propitiation for our sins. (1 John 4:9-10)

How do we know that God loves us? He gave His Son in order that we might have life in Him. Love always means the commitment to meet others' needs, to give life to them even at great cost to ourselves. Anything less than that is less than love, no matter how good it sounds or feels. God tells us that our love relationship with Him did not begin by our loving Him, for we never would have chosen to do that. We are loved only because He loved us and paid the penalty for our sins with the blood of His own Son. True love never depends on the character of the one being loved; it is dependent only on the nature of the lover. It is that way when God loves us, and it is that way when we love one another.

> Beloved, if God so loved us, we also ought to love one another. No one has ever seen God; if we love one another, God abides in us and his love is perfected in us. (1 John 4:11-12)

Adequate!

If God loved us at great cost to Himself and gave even His Son to bear the pain of our sin, then we must never do less with one another and call it love. Never can we give empty words or meaningless actions to another person and say that is love. Love is the giving of ourselves to meet real needs in each other's lives. When that depth of love is shared, the God who is invisible is able to be seen in the way in which we love one another; then a fullness of love is ours which binds us together in every way.

> We love because he first loved us. (1 John 4:19)

We are able to love one another only because God has first loved us, giving us both the capacity to love and the demonstration of how to give that love away. Because God has lavished His love on us by means of His Son, He fully expects us to relate to one another according to the measure of that love. The validity of our relationship with God is either revealed or denied on the basis of the way we love one another.

> If anyone says, "I love God," and hates his brother, he is a liar; for he who does not love his brother whom he has seen cannot love God whom he has not seen. And this commandment we have from him: whoever loves God must also love his brother. (1 John 4:20-21)

What does a "community of servants" look like in real life? The organization that publishes this book *Adequate!*, Leadership Resources International, is actually an organization that began as a "one-to-one" discipleship ministry in 1970 and grew to become a mission focused on equipping and encouraging pastors and church leaders in the developing world. God has graciously given us many staff members who work in our Global Ministry Center in the Chicago area and also several based in other places in the world. Our training teams of national leaders are found in Asia, the South Pacific, Latin America, Africa and Russia.

We know that God has given us this ministry by His mercy and that we have grown not by our dreams and creative training methods, but because God's gracious hand has been on us. But the great blessing of God on us is not seen primarily in the expansion of our work and the opportunity to help many thousands of pastors who might otherwise not have access to training that equips them to study, teach and preach the Scriptures more effectively and to shepherd their people after the Father's heart. God's greater blessing is seen in our relationships, how He has enabled us to walk with one another along the way.

God has by His grace made us a "community of servants" who give ourselves first to our Lord and then to one another and to God's people. We actually live by means of the Scripture passages we have studied here. We love to exalt each other and try to outdo one another in being each other's servant. Sound idealistic? Isn't this what God expects as a norm among His people when His Spirit lives within them and they follow His word?

In reality, we have all hurt each other over the years. We have often said the wrong thing to each other, or said the right thing but in the wrong way. We have sinned against and disappointed each other deeply. But we are committed to bearing with and forgiving each other, walking together in humility, and God's grace has flowed among us and through us to His glory.

Perhaps the most amazing thing about all this is that the stewardship of our relationships is led not by our teachers, but our support staff. We have six staff members who organize, coordinate, and help all the rest of us be successful. Tom Hill, Karen Mills, George Bowater, Gloria Twietmeyer, Gail Jackson and David Horecny know what the heart of God looks like and generously, humbly bring His heart to us in abundance. Maybe God has enriched you in your church or ministry with gifts like these brothers and sisters. What a treasure! The life of God flows from relationships like this, and fill the earth with His glory.

QUESTIONS FOR COMMUNICATION AND APPLICATION

1. What opportunities is God giving you to "wash the feet" of people around you?

2. Do you see the "heart of a servant" expressed in your ministry? What attitudes and responses must change in order for you to express the heart of God in your relationships?

3. In what relationships can you persevere with others and encourage them with the Scriptures in order to bear their weaknesses? How would you do that?

4. Why do we lack the freedom to confess our sins to one another? For that reason, do we miss opportunities to be healed?

But I am afraid that as the serpent deceived Eve by his cunning, your thoughts will be led astray from a sincere and pure devotion to Christ.

2 Corinthians 11:3

7

A Kingdom of Affirmation

We must never be naive; Satan's desire is to destroy us. However, he cannot do so because "for he who is in you is greater than he who is in the world" (1 John 4:4). Satan is our enemy and is continually seeking to steal away our hearts from the Lord. Surprisingly, his most common weapon against us is not in the blatant, brutal frontal attacks, but in developing within us a speculative mind-set about the Scriptures. Satan's realm of darkness is a kingdom of speculations; God's realm of light is a Kingdom of affirmation.

TAKING EVERY THOUGHT CAPTIVE

From his second Corinthian letter, we probably learn more about the apostle Paul and about how he saw himself and the ministry God had given him than in any of his other letters.

> I, Paul, myself entreat you, by the meekness and gentleness of Christ—I who am humble when face to face with you, but bold toward you when I am away!— (2 Corinthians 10:1)

Adequate!

Paul is quoting here what many in the Corinthian church were saying about him. You can almost hear them: "When Paul is present with us he is such a warm and gentle fellow. But when he goes away and writes us a letter, he comes on strong!"

> I do not want to appear to be frightening you with my letters. For they say, "His letters are weighty and strong, but his bodily presence is weak, and his speech of no account." (2 Corinthians 10:9-10)

Paul was probably not a very eloquent speaker and probably not very attractive according to this world's fleshly standards. Apart from the sovereignty of God, he might have had a difficult time being a success in this time of electronic media. I can relate to Paul! A few years ago I was in California for a Bible conference. During one of the breaks, a gracious lady came up to me and said, "I want you to know that listening to you is just like listening to Jesus." Of course, I turned around to see who she was talking to!

God has a wonderful way of balancing these things out. When I was back in California a few weeks later for another conference, a college student who sat in the front row, had not said much to me. After the conference was over, he came to me and said, "I want you to know how much it means to me to see the Lord using you." I started to say, "Thank you," but he continued. "You know, you're really not a very good speaker. You don't have a very good personality, and you're not even very good looking. I want you to know what an encouragement it is to me to see God using someone so ordinary." I have to respond to both of those comments in the same way. "You know who I am, Lord, and it does not make much difference how people see me." That is probably how Paul felt as he received this feedback from the Corinthian church.

> I beg of you that when I am present I may not have to show boldness with such confidence as I count on showing against some

who suspect us of walking according to the flesh. For though we walk in the flesh, we are not waging war according to the flesh. For the weapons of our warfare are not of the flesh but have divine power to destroy strongholds. (2 Corinthians 10:2-4)

Paul's resources in ministry were not of this world, nor were his weapons of the flesh. He had placed no confidence in his own strength, his persuasiveness or his eloquence. His weapons against the enemies of darkness were the knowledge of God and a heart of obedience to Christ.

We destroy arguments and every lofty opinion raised against the knowledge of God, and take every thought captive to obey Christ, being ready to punish every disobedience, when your obedience is complete. (2 Corinthians 10:5-6)

Paul's preaching was aimed at destroying arguments and lofty opinions or "speculations" against the knowledge of God. These battles in our personal lives, our relationships and our ministries are won by taking every thought captive to the obedience of Christ. On one hand we see the great apostle's desire for all of life and ministry: the knowledge of God. Paul had said to the church at Philippi, "I want to know Christ" (Philippians 3:10). That knowledge was the consuming desire of his heart. It was also his desire in ministry to bring everyone he met to the knowledge of God. On the other hand, Paul talked about the lofty, speculative things raised from the minds of men and women. Paul sees his life purpose as the destruction of those pretensions and speculations, as he takes every thought captive to the obedience of Christ, resulting in the knowledge of God.

The weapons we use in ministry do not come from us. They are God's alone. His truth, His Spirit and His power destroy the strongholds of the enemy. We have already talked about the weapon of prayer in spiritual warfare. Our enemies have set up fortresses in our rights and pleasures, in our pursuit of things, in religious and political systems and false teachings about world views, and the worship of false gods. We are called to participate with God in the demolishing of those strongholds through the teaching of the Scripture, in prayer, and in the obedience of our hearts. This ministry of power and authority is what Satan seeks to steal away from us, and replace it with a mind-set of speculations.

DESTROYING SPECULATIONS

We see our enemy's battle strategy from the very beginning. When Satan was tempting Eve, he was leading her to speculate on what God had said.

> The LORD God commanded the man, saying, "You may surely eat of every tree of the garden, but of the tree of the knowledge of good and evil you shall not eat, for in the day that you eat of it you shall surely die." (Genesis 2:16-17)

However, Satan said as he came to Eve:

> Did God actually say, "You shall not eat of any tree in the garden"? (Genesis 3:1b)

"Could it be that God is holding something back from you that would be a means of growth for you? Why is God keeping you from something good? You can know what God knows and you can be like God if you eat this fruit." Satan is causing Eve to speculate about what God has said, and in the environment of those speculations, he is leading her astray to disobedience.

We see this same strategy from the enemy as Moses is standing before the burning bush. God is calling Moses to obedience and to ministry, but Satan is right there to put all the speculations and "what if" questions in his mind. As we read God's call to

Moses in Exodus three and four, we see Moses' responses characterized by "Who am I..."; "Suppose I do and..."; "What if they do not believe me or listen..."; "O Lord, I have never been eloquent..."; "O Lord, please send someone else to do it." Satan is stealing away from Moses a whole heart of obedience through the speculations he brings.

We see Satan using the same strategy with Christ in the temptation in the wilderness. Luke records this battle in chapter 4 of his Gospel. "If you are the Son of God, tell this stone to become bread. If you are really God's child, would He allow you to be starving here in the wilderness?" What is wrong with turning stones into bread? In an environment of speculations the enemy seeks to steal away obedience from Jesus. "If you are the Son of God, throw yourself down from here. God has already promised that He will send His angels to catch you, hasn't he?" "Speculations" has been the battle strategy of our enemy from the very beginning.

Paul laid out this truth about the vulnerability of man's heart and mind as he began his letter to Rome. In this passage Paul sets before us something of a history of man in relationship with God, and we see the battle of the ages.

> The wrath of God is revealed from heaven against all ungodliness and unrighteousness of men, who by their unrighteousness suppress the truth. For what can be known about God is plain to them, because God has shown it to them. For his invisible attributes, namely, his eternal power and divine nature, have been clearly perceived, ever since the creation of the world, in the things that have been made. So they are without excuse. (Romans 1:18-20)

No man or woman can ever stand before God with an excuse for failing to worship Him. He has clearly revealed Himself in His creation. God has made the knowledge of Himself plain from the very beginning.

Although they knew God, they did not honor him as God or give thanks to him, but they became futile in their thinking, and their foolish hearts were darkened. Claiming to be wise, they became fools, and exchanged the glory of the immortal God for images resembling mortal man and birds and animals and reptiles. (Romans 1:21-23)

When God revealed Himself in all His creation and made visible the things concerning Him, He was calling all mankind to worship Him. Rather than worshiping God in light of the knowledge He gave to us, we suppressed the truth. We elevated ourselves and the things that fill our own minds, and in that process we became futile in our thinking. As we congratulated ourselves on our wisdom and accomplishments, we began to live as fools. This is what Satan has been seeking from the very beginning, causing us to reject God and His truth, to exalt our own minds and our own accomplishments, and to pursue our own way rather than the glory of God.

Paul begins his first letter to Timothy with this warning:

As I urged you when I was going to Macedonia, remain at Ephesus that you may charge certain persons not to teach any different doctrine, nor to devote themselves to myths and endless genealogies, which promote speculations rather than the stewardship from God that is by faith. (1 Timothy 1:3-4)

Paul clearly contrasts a whole heart of obedience with a mind-set of speculations. While God is calling us to respond with a whole heart of faith when He speaks His Word to us, there is always a vulnerability instead to focus on "myths and endless genealogies." We tend to become caught up in the speculations and the controversial things, to respond only with our minds to the things we are hearing.

VACILLATIONS AND THE FLESH

Paul began his second Corinthian letter with some excellent teaching on decision making. If you have difficulty making decisions and discerning the will of God, I hope that this Scripture verse will be a great encouragement to your heart.

> Our boast is this: the testimony of our conscience that we behaved in the world with simplicity and godly sincerity, not by earthly wisdom but by the grace of God, and supremely so toward you. (2 Corinthians 1:12)

Paul lays before the church at Corinth the basis for his confidence as a man and as a minister. He did not conduct himself personally or in his ministry on the basis of fleshly or worldly wisdom, but in holiness and godly sincerity. His heart was whole and pure before the Lord and before the Corinthians.

> Because I was sure of this, I wanted to come to you first, so that you might have a second experience of grace. I wanted to visit you on my way to Macedonia, and to come back to you from Macedonia and have you send me on my way to Judea. Was I vacillating when I wanted to do this? Do I make my plans according to the flesh, ready to say "Yes, yes" and "No, no" at the same time? (2 Corinthians 1:15-17)

In this passage, Paul is sharing with the church at Corinth that he made a decision, believing that God was leading him to go to Macedonia. Thus, he sent word to the church at Corinth and said, "Why don't I stop and visit you on the way to Macedonia and stop on the way back again. I can be a blessing to you twice. [Paul was such a confident man!] Then you can also help me on my journey to Judea." As it turned out, God led Paul another way. Because of the difficulty some of the brothers and sisters in the church at Corinth had with Paul in response to his confrontational letters, it seems that Paul felt he had to defend this decision. These people might even have subtly communicated that Paul, as the great apostle who is always telling them how to run their church, somehow missed God's leading and will in this matter. Paul gives this wonderfully graphic picture of vacillating in his response to them.

> As surely as God is faithful, our word to you has not been Yes and No. For the Son of God, Jesus Christ, whom we proclaimed among you, Silvanus and Timothy and I, was not Yes and No, but in him it is always Yes. For all the promises of God find their Yes in him. That is why it is through him that we utter our Amen to God for his glory. (2 Corinthians 1:18-20)

Paul returned to the basis of his confidence—that he conducted his life and ministry in holiness and godly sincerity, not in fleshly wisdom. He did not depend on his abilities to figure out the best thing to do in any given situation, nor how to cause people to respond, nor how to bring about the results he desired. He came before the Lord with a whole heart, praying that God would lead him; then he walked in confidence believing that God was leading him. He did not vacillate in the process, experiencing the "yes, yes, no, no" that the enemy and our flesh bring to confuse us.

DECISIONS AND THE WILL OF GOD

Have you ever been confronted with a significant decision in your life, perhaps concerning a major purchase, the direction of a relationship, an employment choice or a potential ministry? While you were thinking and praying about it, talking to people and seeking their counsel, you might have said, "I really think that this is what God wants me to do." Then you thought about it more, prayed a little more, talked to a few more people and said,

"No, I think probably I should go this other direction." Then a few days later, "No, I think I was really right the first time." Back and forth we go, vacillating in the process. Paul did not do that, and we can experience that same confidence and freedom. We, too, can come to God with whole hearts, seeking His leading, and then walk boldly in His will.

We are so vulnerable, however, to vacillations. Satan is seeking to steal away our freedom to walk with God confidently in life and ministry in that vacillation process.

I had a common, frustrating experience not long ago when I walked into a pastor's office and saw on his desk a booklet titled, *How to Discover the Will of God.* I always respond with great difficulty in my heart when I see something like that because God never talks to us about His will as something "we discover," something we "find out." God always speaks about His will as something we are found in. God's will is that which He works out in our lives as we walk with Him. The picture of us as "rats in a maze" is one in which we take all the right turns at the right time and go through all the open doors, never trying to force the closed doors open. If we do that often enough, one day we will come to the place in which we have "discovered God's will for our lives."

A young person with all the big, heavy questions for her life might be asking, "Should I go to college? What should I study? Should I prepare for the mission field? Whom should I marry?" Then one dark night lightning strikes, and she has all the answers to the big questions for her life. She has discovered God's will! That is such foolishness! We are not playing a game of hide and seek with God. He is a God of revelation; He opens Himself to be known. He calls us to come to Himself with responsive hearts and takes us from that place, fulfilling all His will in our lives. That is the very freedom Satan is trying to steal away from us in the speculations, the "what if" questions and the "should have" feelings.

When God sets an opportunity before us, Satan immediately brings to our minds a myriad of "what if" questions. "If I move to that city, what if my family doesn't like it there? What if people don't respond? What if I don't have enough money?" We go there with some very real hopes mixed with the fears; when it does not work out exactly the way we had hoped, Satan gets us on the other side with the "should haves." It is then that we say, "I should have done something else." There is no freedom to walk with God in that process. However, when we come to Him with responsive hearts, He leads us and fulfills all His will in our lives.

Paul is such a great example of this freedom to walk confidently with God as He fulfills His will through us. Paul was the kind of man who always seemed to have a sense of what God was doing. Even before he was born again, he "knew" that God had raised him up to destroy this new sect of believers in Jesus. While he was on the way to bring destruction to the Church, God transformed his life. After his conversion and a time of discipleship with the Lord in the wilderness, it is as if Paul said, "I know exactly what God is doing. He has raised me up to minister to the Jews. There is no one more perfect for this ministry than I. I know them. I am one of them. I am one of their leaders; I know the Law, and they respect me. I can see what God is doing." When he tried to fulfill that ministry, he had to be let down over a wall in the middle of the night to save his life from the persecutors. Paul would go to one city trying to minister, and he would be stoned along the way. He would go to another place and would be shipwrecked trying to get there. He would approach another city only to be persecuted. In another place he would face starvation. Finally he would arrive in a city in which people were willing to listen to him and what would he say? "God led me here!" From a human perspective, Paul's ministry appears completely haphazard, with no pattern whatsoever. But God was leading and fulfilling His sovereign will in His apostle's life.

God's will is what He is working out in our lives as we walk with Him. There is no pressure to "get it right." Our ability to "discover God's will" is never the issue; the heart with which we come before Him is always the issue. When we come to God with a whole heart, desiring to do His will, pursuing His glory and praying that He will lead us, we can walk boldly and confidently with Him. Even if things do not work out the way we had hoped, our hearts are still free. With Paul we can say, "God led me." It is that confidence to walk boldly that Satan is trying to steal away from us amidst the speculations. He is always pressuring us, telling us that if we make a wrong choice or if we fail to see God's will clearly, our lives and our ministries will never be the same. But our freedom is grounded in a sovereign God who fulfills all His will, even with ordinary people who come to Him with a whole heart.

REBUKE AND FORGIVE

I want to look with you at another passage in which we see our enemy using a mind-set of speculations to steal a heart of obedience away from us.

> He said to his disciples, "Temptations to sin are sure to come, but woe to the one through whom they come! It would be better for him if a millstone were hung around his neck and he were cast into the sea than that he should cause one of these little ones to sin." (Luke 17:1-2)

Jesus is preparing His disciples for ministry. He desires them to walk with a sense of reality and with their eyes wide open. He does not want them to be naive about the life to which He has called them. The truth is, this life is filled with stumbling blocks; we are continually confronted with people who cause others to sin. God has called us to be stepping stones in one another's lives, a means of encouragement. There is a strong warning here for the person who becomes a stumbling block. For the person who causes another to sin, Jesus says that it is much better for him—not just the people he is causing to stumble—to have a millstone hung around his neck and to be thrown into the sea. The Lord of the Church has a great commitment to wholeness in relationships, and we must reflect that truth in our lives together.

> Pay attention to yourselves! If your brother sins, rebuke him, and if he repents, forgive him, and if he sins against you seven times in the day, and turns to you seven times, saying, "I repent," you must forgive him. (Luke 17:3-4)

Jesus then gave His disciples instructions for dealing with sin in relationships. Stumbling blocks will come and bring great pain in our relationships with one another. When brothers or sisters sin against you, you must rebuke and then forgive them—even if it happens over and over again the same day. We read this and think immediately of the companion passage in Matthew 18, in which Peter came to Jesus:

> Peter came up and said to him, "Lord, how often will my brother sin against me, and I forgive him? As many as seven times?" (Matthew 18:21)

We know that seven is a big number in Peter's mind. You can almost hear him saying, "Lord, how often should my brother do the same thing and still I must respond with forgiveness? Isn't there a time to talk about forgiveness and then a time to talk about my brother's responsibility to me?" Jesus then says:

Jesus said to him, "I do not say to you seven times, but seventy times seven." (Matthew 18:22)

And we know that Jesus is not saying, "Peter, keep track and when you reach 490 times, that is enough." Peter is talking about limits, and Jesus takes away all the limits! There is no limit to the forgiveness of God in the lives of His children, and there must be no limit to our forgiveness of one another. It is always the law that is measured out carefully. The law is always saying, "How far do I have to go; how much is enough?" Love never asks that question, because love is never measured out carefully. Love is always poured out.

We have great difficulty with forgiveness. Whenever a member of our own family or a member of our greater family in the church hurts us and the wound is open and alive to pain, it is only by the mercy of God that we can forgive. Only by applying His healing love to that place in our relationship can we forgive.

But as much difficulty as we have with forgiveness, we have even more difficulty with rebuking. There is not much rebuking taking place in the Body of Christ anymore because Satan has convinced us that our relationships are very fragile. If we say the wrong thing or if there is a deep disagreement or failure, it will never be the same. Satan is trying to steal away from us the very thing God uses to cleanse, heal, and deepen our commitment to one another in the Church. We need far more freedom to rebuke one another than we have. There are no fragile relationships in the Body of Christ. We can go through anything with one another, and as we respond the way God teaches us and enables us, our relationships will be even deeper than they were before. How do the disciples respond to this teaching?

INCREASE OUR FAITH?

The apostles said to the Lord, "Increase our faith!" (Luke 17:5)

The world can hardly contain the books that have been written and the sermons that have been preached on this verse. How wonderful for the disciples to come to Jesus and say, "Increase our faith!" We can hardly imagine a more spiritual response. Does Jesus affirm their hunger for more faith?

> And the Lord said, "If you had faith like a grain of mustard seed, you could say to this mulberry tree, 'Be uprooted and planted in the sea,' and it would obey you." (Luke 17:6)

That is an interesting response! The disciples ask the Lord for more faith and He talks about faith like a mustard seed producing great power. In fact, Jesus is talking about trees obeying the disciples if they have faith. How big is a mustard seed? It is so small it is almost insignificant in its measure. Jesus tells them that if they had faith like that, trees would obey them.

> Will any one of you who has a servant plowing or keeping sheep say to him when he has come in from the field, "Come at once and recline at table"? Will he not rather say to him, "Prepare supper for me, and dress properly, and serve me while I eat and drink, and afterward you will eat and drink"? Does he thank the servant because he did what was commanded? So you also, when you have done all that you were commanded, say, "We are unworthy servants; we have only done what was our duty." (Luke 17:7-10)

As Jesus is teaching the disciples, they can visualize this scene clearly because the slave and the master were so much a part of their culture. They knew the servant went out in the morning even before dawn, so that he could be in the field at first light. He would work all day and give his strength, his heart, and his time for the enrichment of his master. At the end of the day he would return exhausted, hungry and thirsty. What had the master been doing all the time that the slave has been out in the field? He had probably been going over his books, spending time with his wife and visiting with the other important men in the city.

Now when the slave comes in at the end of the day, does the master look at him and say, "I've been getting rich all day at your expense. You're tired and hungry. Now it is my turn. Why don't you take a shower, and while you are resting, I'll fix your dinner." No, that is not what happens. When the slave comes in from the field at the end of the day, the master says, "Prepare my dinner, draw my bath, and after you have taken care of every whim and desire I have, you can take care of yourself." He does not even thank the servant for what he has done. Why? That is the nature of the relationship between the master and his slave.

WHO IS THE MASTER?

Why would Jesus tell His disciples this story at this point in His ministry? Do you realize what has taken place in this passage? Jesus is preparing His disciples for the ministry of His life and the building of the church. As He is preparing them, He warns them about stumbling blocks in relationships and calls them to rebuke and to forgive. How do the disciples respond to Jesus? Do they say, "Yes, Lord, that's what we will do"? No. They turn it around, giving Him a command to obey by saying, "Increase our faith." They have become confused in their relationship with the Lord about who is the master and who is the servant.

Sometimes in our relationship with God we, too, become confused about who is the master and who is the servant. We even see this truth revealed in our prayer meetings. What tends to characterize our prayer lives? "Lord, my aunt is sick in the hospital; would you heal her? Lord, my children are struggling in school, would you help them? Lord, my husband is having a difficulty with his boss, would you work things out for him? My wife is depressed, would you lift her spirits? Lord, my church needs leadership, would you provide that? Lord, we need wisdom for this ministry, would you give it? Lord, would you provide these finances?" Lord, do this. Lord, do that. While we must never take anything away from the freedom we have as the children of God to bring every need and request of our hearts to Him, when giving direction to our Father consumes our prayer lives, something is out of proportion. Often we, too, become confused in our relationship with God about who is the master that gives direction, and who is the servant that responds in obedience.

At times even our correct theology brings vulnerability in this battle. We see God as sovereign. He has all creation under His control and can do anything He desires to do. He can speak a word and His will is done. Sometimes rather than this truth creating worship in our hearts, causing us to stand in awe and reverence before God, a great frustration develops in the midst of overwhelming circumstances and pain. "Well, God, if you have the power to make these things right, why aren't you doing it?" In that process the Lord God, the Holy One who reigns forever and ever, becomes reduced to our all-powerful servant in the sky. We become the ones who give direction, and we expect Him to respond in obedience to what we ask of Him.

Most of us have our lives well planned. Almost every one of us has a rather clear sense of what we would like to see happen in the next five years in our marriages, our families, our ministries, and our churches. We have a clear vision of what we would like God to do. So much of our relationship with God is characterized by bringing all those things to Him and expecting Him to work them out. That often becomes our view of Him. Sometimes, like the disciples, we see ourselves out of proportion in our relationship with God, and we become confused about who is the one who gives direction and who is the one who responds in obedience.

In the amazing way that Jesus wove together His words and His works, He now brings the disciples into a real life situation where they can see what He desires to teach them.

> On the way to Jerusalem he was passing along between Samaria and Galilee. And as he entered a village, he was met by ten lepers, who stood at a distance and lifted up their voices, saying, "Jesus, Master, have mercy on us." (Luke 17:11-13)

Do you think it is insignificant that the lepers call Him Master? The disciples in the inner circle, the "professional Christians," seem to see Him as something less than master. That is why Jesus told them the story of the master and his servant. However, these ten lepers who stand at a distance see Him for who He is and call Him Lord.

> When he saw them he said to them, "Go and show yourselves to the priests." (Luke 17:14a)

Because of society's great fear of the contagion of leprosy, lepers lived together in isolated colonies. If a leper felt he had been healed or cleansed, he would go and show himself to the priests who would either say, "You are still a leper, go back to the leper colony," or, "Yes, you are healed, you can come back into town." Now we hear these lepers crying out to Jesus, "Master have mercy on us." Jesus responds, "Go, show yourselves to the priests."

Would it not be understandable for one of the lepers to put up his hand and say, "Jesus, aren't we getting something out of order here? First, you have to heal us, and then we will show ourselves to the priests. If we go and show ourselves to the priests now, we're still lepers and will look like fools. First you heal us; then we show ourselves to the priests." The lepers knew something about Jesus that the disciples had not yet learned. A servant is permitted only one response in relationship to his master, and that response is never "Yes, if," or "Yes, but," or "Yes, when." The only response that is permitted is, "Yes, Lord."

And as they went they were cleansed. (Luke 17:14b)

In the environment of their obedience God healed their lives!

Then one of them, when he saw that he was healed, turned back, praising God with a loud voice; and he fell on his face at Jesus' feet, giving him thanks. Now he was a Samaritan. (Luke 17:15-16)

We know Jesus is not going to pass up an opportunity to comment on this. The only one of the ten who came back with a heart of gratitude was a Samaritan. The one that so many of God's people despised came back with a heart of worship.

Jesus answered, "Were not ten cleansed? Where are the nine? Was no one found to return and give praise to God except this foreigner?" And he said to him, "Rise and go your way; your faith has made you well." (Luke 17:17-19)

SPECULATION OR OBEDIENCE

The disciples had said to Jesus, "Increase our faith." Now Jesus says to the leper, "Your faith has made you well." What kind of faith did the leper express? Was he the visionary in the back of the congregational meeting who spoke of the great dreams and ideals God was setting before the people? That is how we tend to see faith. Was he the one encouraging all the people of God: "God will provide for us; we need to trust Him in this." No, all this leper did was what God told him to do. Jesus is defining faith for His disciples. It is not centered in vision and dreams; faith is a heart of obedience before the Lord. We can hear Jesus saying to His disciples, "Do what I tell you to do, and I will call you men of great faith." Faith is never a mechanism we use to move God to do something for us. Rather, faith is always the means God uses to cause us to be obedient to Him.

There is such a contrast between the disciples and the lepers! When Jesus gave the disciples a command to obey, they responded by speculating about it. We can hear the disciples saying, "Lord, we know that what you are telling us is the right thing to do. Although we want to live like that, we are not ready yet. We cannot rebuke, forgive, or confront in that way yet. We are not mature enough, nor do we know the Scriptures well enough; we do not have enough faith. As soon as you give us all the faith we need, we will be more than happy to obey you." These are the speculations the enemy brings! It all sounds so right. What could possibly be more mature and more spiritual than asking God for more faith? Yet nothing could be further from what God had set before them!

How we love to speculate! We love to sit in our Bible study groups and our classes and deal with the Scriptures with our minds rather than with our hearts. "What would that thought mean over in this situation, or how would this concept apply over here? What would it look like in that circumstance, or how does this relate to this over here?" The whole experience is often only a mental exercise. We love to digress from the heart of the text and talk about all these implications. Sometimes we leave our church services saying to the pastor, "You really gave me something to think about today," as if God had any real interest in expanding our insights. God desires to transform our values, our motives, our priorities, our pursuits and our passions. So often we re-

Adequate!

spond as the disciples did. We have developed a way of responding to the Scriptures with our minds alone, and in this process truth does not transform our hearts. God calls us to obedience, just as He did His disciples.

SINCERE AND PURE DEVOTION

Return with me once again to Paul's clear contrast in 2 Corinthians 10:

> Though we walk in the flesh, we are not waging war according to the flesh. For the weapons of our warfare are not of the flesh but have divine power to destroy strongholds. We destroy arguments and every lofty opinion raised against the knowledge of God, and take every thought captive to obey Christ. (2 Corinthians 10:3-5)

Notice that these are the mental responses and arguments that come from our minds; they are the pretensions and speculations the enemy brings.

This is the process in which we walk to holiness and to ministry, taking every thought captive to the obedience of Christ! As we studied God's call of Ezekiel earlier, we looked at God's process of preparation for the ministry of His Word. We talked about assimilation, incarnation, and about how the Word must come alive within us before we can teach and minister in power and authority. We saw how Jesus became obedient to the point of death, even death on a cross, and the Word became flesh and dwelt among us. We discussed how our response of obedience to the Word of God is the heart of this process. This is the same truth Paul is setting before us now. In the process of obedience the Word of God comes alive in our hearts, grows to fruitfulness and prepares us to walk with God in ministry. It is in our obedience that Satan is defeated.

We can visualize a woman struggling with her marriage. Perhaps she is hurting in a pain-filled and competitive relationship. God calls her to a spirit of submission and says, "He may be won over without words by your behavior" (1 Peter 3:1-2). How often might she respond, "But God, you do not know my husband. If I do that, who knows what he might ask me to do." Satan is stealing away from her a heart of obedience in the midst of all the "what ifs," the "should haves" and the speculations.

We can hear God talking to a man about his priorities, about how he spends his money, his time and the resources of his heart. God says, "I want you to orient every resource around my church and around the building of my Kingdom." Satan is right there. "But what if I do that and I don't have enough money for this, or what if I can't keep doing these things I love?" A servant is permitted only one response in relationship to the master. "Yes, Lord." As we take every thought captive to obedience, God's Word comes alive within us and grows to fruitfulness; then it overflows from us in a ministry of fruitfulness, to the glory of God. In chapter 11, Paul comes back to these same things:

> I wish you would bear with me in a little foolishness. Do bear with me! I feel a divine jealousy for you, for I betrothed you to one husband, to present you as a pure virgin to Christ. But I am afraid that as the serpent deceived Eve by his cunning, your thoughts will be led astray from a sincere and pure devotion to Christ. (2 Corinthians 11:1-3)

Paul is talking about the "sincere and pure devotion" of our hearts. Sometimes we look at the Christian life as being so mysterious and mystical. We want to walk with God; we want to be used of Him, but we have such a hard time figuring out what it is all about and what we are supposed to do. We are unsure about all the implications of this new life. The Christian life is not really mysterious or mystical at all. God is God, and He is raising us up to be His servants. He leads us by His Spirit, calls us to walk in obedience, and pours His life out through us; His glory fills the earth. Satan is trying to steal away the simplicity and purity of our devotion to Christ.

THE HANDMAID OF THE LORD

Abraham is a wonderful model of what God is setting before us here. God had given him the son of the promise in a miraculous way. When Isaac was still a young man, God said, "Abraham, I want you to sacrifice Isaac to me." What a time for speculations! How could the promises of God be fulfilled if the son of the promise was dead? We read the story and our hearts our wrenched within us. We can see Abraham going through the preparations for the journey, coming to the mountain of sacrifice, and walking up that mountain arm in arm with his son. We know there is a tremendous battle raging in his heart. With all his heart he wants to be a faithful son to his heavenly Father, and at the same time he wants to be a faithful father to his earthly son. He builds the altar and lays the son of his love, the son of the promise, on the altar. Taking out the knife, he is just about to drive the life out of his son when God stops him.

> He said, "Do not lay your hand on the boy or do anything to him, for now I know that you fear God, seeing you have not withheld your son, your only son, from me." (Genesis 22:12)

What a heart of obedience we see in this man of God! That was the day Abraham learned that trusting in the person of God is even better than trusting in the promises of God.

We see this same heart response in Mary, the mother of our Lord Jesus. Do you remember how the angel appeared to her and said, "Mary, you're going to have a baby." Was this good news?

What a time for speculations! She was a virgin; she had never known a man. Although there were some honest questions, do you remember the response of her heart?

> Mary said, "Behold, I am the servant of the Lord; let it be to me according to your word." And the angel departed from her. (Luke 1:38)

This is the heart of obedience that Paul is describing in these Scripture passages—taking every thought captive to obedience, our sincere and pure devotion in the midst of the enemy's speculations. God fills the earth with His glory when ordinary people say yes to Him!

QUESTIONS FOR COMMUNICATION AND APPLICATION

1. How vulnerable are you to Satan's manipulations that cause you to speculate rather than obey?

2. How free do you feel to affirm the will of God in your life and not vacillate with "what ifs" or look back with "should haves"?

3. Does your level of obedience reflect a "purity of devotion" toward the Lord? In what areas of your life can a whole heart of obedience be more clearly seen?

And I heard every creature in heaven and on earth and under the earth and in the sea, and all that is in them, saying, "To him who sits on the throne and to the Lamb be blessing and honor and glory and might forever and ever!"

Revelation 5:13

8
A Royal Priesthood

God has progressively revealed Himself through His creation, His Word, and His Son. After Adam and Eve exchanged the knowledge of God for the knowledge of this realm, they lived in complete darkness. They possessed no ability to know God or His eternal Kingdom. Even though humankind chose to live their lives out of relationship with God, God continued to reveal Himself in order to reconcile man back into relationship with Him. God has revealed Himself in the natural realm; He has written His law in the hearts of men; He has spoken through the patriarchs and the prophets; and He has sent His own Son, who is the fullest revelation of the person of God.

God did not end His work of reconciliation and revelation with the death and resurrection of His Son. He continued to speak His Word through the apostles in order that in the revelation of His Word we might have a complete record of His will for us. Through the death and resurrection of His Son and the filling of the Holy Spirit, God has now many sons and daughters through whom He is pouring out His life in this world. You and I are part of that Body in whom God dwells and through whom He is eternally calling men and women to Himself.

THE MINISTRY OF RECONCILIATION

God is in the process of reconciling the world unto Himself. The great eternal God with all His holiness and righteousness could never be reconciled to the world; He cannot be brought down; He cannot be moved. God brings His children to Himself through His Son, and that is the ministry He has committed to us. After Paul wrote to the Corinthians about the love of Christ which moves us, His goals that become ours, and learning to see people through His eyes, he says,

> All this is from God, who through Christ reconciled us to himself and gave us the ministry of reconciliation; that is, in Christ God was reconciling the world to himself, not counting their trespasses against them, and entrusting to us the message of reconciliation. (2 Corinthians 5:18-19)

You and I are commissioned to bring a rebellious and sinful world to a just and holy God, and we are sent with the words of reconciliation on our lips. We are the chosen vessels through whom God is breaking through the walls that men have built to keep Him away from them; we are the tools He desires to use to bring people back into His love. We stand before men and women in God's place, with His words in our mouths and His love in our hearts to tell them the greatest news in all the world: God has taken our sin and placed it on Christ, and He has taken His righteousness and placed it on us. We are able to stand now in God's presence both clean and free because He has destroyed the barrier of sin and reconciled us to Himself by the blood of the cross.

We are ambassadors for Christ, God making his appeal through us. We implore you on behalf of Christ, be reconciled to God. For our sake he made him to be sin who knew no sin, so that in him we might become the righteousness of God. (2 Corinthians 5:20-21)

The proclamation of this message was committed to the disciples by the authority of the risen and exalted Lord. We have been commissioned with them in the ministry of making disciples of Christ, teaching them to live obedient lives by the power of the Holy Spirit.

Jesus came and said to them, "All authority in heaven and on earth has been given to me. Go therefore and make disciples of all nations, baptizing them in the name of the Father and of the Son and of the Holy Spirit, teaching them to observe all that I have commanded you. And behold, I am with you always, to the end of the age." (Matthew 28:18-20)

PROCLAIMING THE PERSON OF GOD

God has called us not only as reconcilers but also to be His priests. He has chosen us as a people in His sovereign will, caused us to be holy by His righteous love, through the blood of His own Son, and by His mercy has made us His own children. We are priests who call people to a Holy God, and our ministry is proclaiming to the world the excellencies of God's person and character. Through lives of holiness, compelled by the love of Jesus, faithfully bringing the Scriptures, we lift before the people around us how big, how beautiful and how good is our God.

You are a chosen race, a royal priesthood, a holy nation, a people for his own possession, that you may proclaim the excellencies of him who called you out of darkness into his marvelous light. Once you were not a people, but now you are God's people; once you had not received mercy, but now you have received mercy. (1 Peter 2:9-10)

[Jesus] made us a kingdom, priests to his God and Father, to him be glory and dominion forever and ever. Amen. (Revelation 1:6)

A priest ministers before God and people in such a way that He is glorified and they are cleansed and sanctified. God has made us His own in order that we might be His vessels for purifying people and setting them aside for Himself. However, a priest's ministry is primarily to God, not to people. God has made us priests to Himself. All of ministry is primarily directed to God and is beneficial to people as an overflow of His love. It is beyond our comprehension that our sins could be removed from God's eternal memory, but even more amazing that God is moved first for His own name and His glory.

I, I am he who blots out your transgressions for my own sake, and I will not remember your sins. (Isaiah 43:25)

When Israel failed to be the people God had called them to be in this world, God promised that He would change them by the power of His Spirit. It is clear that the primary motivation for this ministry was that God's name might be honored among the nations.

Say to the house of Israel, Thus says the Lord GOD: It is not for your sake, O house of Israel, that I am about to act, but for the sake of my holy name, which you have profaned among the nations to which you came. And I will vindicate the holiness of my great name, which has been profaned among the nations, and which you have profaned among them. And the nations will know that I am the LORD, declares the Lord GOD, when through you I vindicate my holiness before their eyes. (Ezekiel 36:22-23)

You and I have been called to proclaim to the world who God is. We are here in order that His name might be honored and glorified, that the world might know Him and give to Him the worship He deserves. We live in a world devastated by pain and injustice. Although we see people everywhere crushed in the pressures of this world and enslaved by their sin, the needs of people will never be sufficient to move us in ministry. Only the glory of God is able to do that. He has made us His priests in order that we might proclaim His excellence before the nations and show forth both the power and glory of the name of the Lord in their midst.

A PROPHETIC ALTERNATIVE

We see this same truth revealed in Paul's letter to the church at Philippi. The way of life God had entrusted to them was in complete contrast with this world so His glory might be seen.

> Do all things without grumbling or questioning, that you may be blameless and innocent, children of God without blemish in the midst of a crooked and twisted generation, among whom you shine as lights in the world, holding fast to the word of life, so that in the day of Christ I may be proud that I did not run in vain or labor in vain. (Philippians 2:14-16)

Christ Himself had taught His disciples that because of His life within them, they were now "salt and light" within this world.

> You are the salt of the earth, but if salt has lost its taste, how shall its saltiness be restored? It is no longer good for anything except to be thrown out and trampled under people's feet. You are the light of the world. A city set on a hill cannot be hidden. Nor do people light a lamp and put it under a basket, but on a stand, and it gives light to all in the house. In the same way, let your light shine before others, so that they may see your good

works and give glory to your Father who is in heaven. (Matthew 5:13-16)

We are commanded to let the light of God shine freely through us in the darkness of this world and to be the salt of the earth. Salt arrests corruption; light exposes what is in the darkness. Just as the prophets called God's people to respond to the Lord, He has placed us here to call a world to Himself. With our mouths we are to proclaim and with our lives we are to be the demonstration of the people God desires us to be; we are to live in such a way that as the world watches, they can understand who God is and what He is like.

If we fail to live out our ministry as salt and light, the world will not learn through us what God is like; as we live out what we have become in Christ, the attributes of God will become visible to them. By watching us, they will see righteousness and justice in all our relationships, mercy and compassion surrounding our families, God's grace and forgiveness shared with one another in our churches. They will see us preferring one another in contrast to competition and selfishness; they will see God's own heart expressed as they watch us give to one another the material things we need. They will see His holiness in the purity of our hearts. God will reveal to the world what He is like by the life He has placed within us.

He has told you, O man, what is good; and what does the LORD require of you but to do justice, and to love kindness, and to walk humbly with your God? (Micah 6:8)

Prophetic voices are critically needed today, before our churches and before the world. God has always raised up His choice vessels to communicate to His people the way in which they ought to live in His presence and before the watching world. We need men and women today who will call the Body of Christ to express the fullness of our lives in Christ in every area, to walk in holiness, and to continually shine God's light on the world of darkness which is blinded to justice, righteousness, and compassion. Children are murdered for the sake of convenience; people are reduced to objects for pleasure; the dignity of multitudes is lost through a lack of compassion; lives are destroyed because of a failure to exercise righteousness and justice. We need to cry out to the world with God's voice that these things must end! We must demonstrate in our churches the hope of an alternative to the realm of death, a place where God's life is freely given to all.

The children of Israel had completely lost their vision of what God had called them to be within this world. Their hearts were far from Him, but they continued to go through the motions of their religious activities. The meaningless forms of their festivals and their empty sacrifices were repulsive to the Lord God. His call to them is a message to the church today as well.

> I hate, I despise your feasts, and I take no delight in your solemn assemblies. Even though you offer me your burnt offerings and grain offerings, I will not accept them; and the peace offerings of your fattened animals, I will not look upon them. Take away from me the noise of your songs; to the melody of your harps I will not listen. But let justice roll down like waters, and righteousness like an ever-flowing stream. (Amos 5:21-24)

LOVE THAT VALIDATES MINISTRY

The very heart of the prophetic voice with which we speak before the world is the way we love one another. Christ taught His disciples that the world would know that they came from Him by the way in which they loved one another.

> A new commandment I give to you, that you love one another: just as I have loved you, you also are to love one another. By this

all people will know that you are my disciples, if you have love for one another. (John 13:34-35)

The world will know that the source of our lives is the Person of God as we love one another with His committed, giving love. That love is the clearest and most visible expression of the reality of His life. From 1 John 4, we have already dealt with the fact that God loves us because He gave us His Son. God's love is always expressed in the giving of life to meet needs.

> By this we know love, that he laid down his life for us, and we ought to lay down our lives for the brothers. But if anyone has the world's goods and sees his brother in need, yet closes his heart against him, how does God's love abide in him? Little children, let us not love in word or talk but in deed and in truth. (1 John 3:16-18)

It is this love which communicates commitment, something of which this world knows so little. The world understands concepts such as using, meeting half way, competing and seeking relationships based on beauty, performance or money. When the world sees the commitment of life to meet needs, the giving of self expecting nothing in return, they know that the source of that love is not this world. The invisible God becomes visible in the way we love one another. The most powerful communication of the Person of God to the world around us is not in the words we speak—it is in the relationships which we share.

> I do not ask for these only, but also for those who will believe in me through their word, that they may all be one, just as you, Father, are in me, and I in you, that they also may be in us, so that the world may believe that you have sent me. (John 17:20-21)

We must know not only that our identity as God's children is at stake in the way we love one another, but also that the great reality of Christ's relationship with His Father becomes clear in the unity of our hearts.

> The glory that you have given me I have given to them, that they may be one even as we are one, I in them and you in me, that they may become perfectly one, so that the world may know that you sent me and loved them even as you loved me. (John 17:22-23)

The great mystery of the unity of the Godhead, the intimacy and depth of life shared, now include God's children as well. The way we live out that unity in relationship with God and one another causes the world to see that Christ really did come forth from God. We mirror the trinity in our relationships of intimacy, love and joy. If our message is just that of words, doctrines, creeds, and codes of ethics, it will be void of the powerful, drawing force of love that is shared. As we love one another with the commitment and life-giving love of God, and as we live together with a unity that cannot be broken, the world will know that we come from Christ, and that Christ came from the Father.

WORKING TOGETHER WITH HIM

God could demonstrate His Person and His love to people in any way He desired. He could form messages with the clouds, send angels to proclaim His Word, or cause the rocks to cry out in praise to Him. However, God has chosen to reveal Himself through His Son and through the church which is His Body. He has made us His co-workers.

> Working together with him, then, we appeal to you not to receive the grace of God in vain. For he says, "In a favorable time I listened to you, and in a day of salvation I have helped you." Behold, now is the favorable time; behold, now is the day of salvation. (2 Corinthians 6:1-2)

Adequate!

God has called us to proclaim to the world that now is the time to respond to His grace, today is the day to receive His life. We speak this message with a sense of meekness and with the heart of a servant, even in the midst of great hardships.

> We put no obstacle in anyone's way, so that no fault may be found with our ministry, but as servants of God we commend ourselves in every way: by great endurance, in afflictions, hardships, calamities, beatings, imprisonments, riots, labors, sleepless nights, hunger; (2 Corinthians 6:3-5)

God has made the character of the messenger consistent with the message itself. And since we have no resources to fulfill what only God can do, we have become completely dependent on Him and on those things that fulfill ministry in a spiritual realm.

> [And we commend ourselves] by purity, knowledge, patience, kindness, the Holy Spirit, genuine love; by truthful speech, and the power of God; with the weapons of righteousness for the right hand and for the left; (2 Corinthians 6:6-7)

People respond to us in many different ways, and even our own feelings fluctuate as we experience that paradox of life and death together. But still our hearts are filled with the joy of knowing God, and possessing what we have in Him.

> [And] through honor and dishonor, through slander and praise. We are treated as impostors, and yet are true; as unknown, and yet well known; as dying, and behold, we live; as punished, and yet not killed; as sorrowful, yet always rejoicing; as poor, yet making many rich; as having nothing, yet possessing everything. (2 Corinthians 6:8-10)

God has called us to speak freely with hearts opened wide, filled with God's love and willing to be emptied. As our hearts are broken with God's compassion for people, we entreat them to respond to us and to the Lord.

We have spoken freely to you, Corinthians; our heart is wide open. You are not restricted by us, but you are restricted in your own affections. In return (I speak as to children) widen your hearts also. (2 Corinthians 6:11-13)

Our passions and desires are focused on the day when we gather with the elders, with God's angels, with every living creature to sing praise to the Father and His exalted Son.

They sang a new song, saying, "Worthy are you to take the scroll and to open its seals, for you were slain, and by your blood you ransomed people for God from every tribe and language and people and nation, and you have made them a kingdom and priests to our God, and they shall reign on the earth." (Revelation 5:9-10)

Every time we respond to God in obedience, each time we speak forth God's life-giving Word, He is using us to prepare for this day. We stand in awe of our great God who has used very ordinary people to fulfill every purpose of His heart and has gained for Himself the worship of all His creation for all eternity.

Then I looked, and I heard around the throne and the living creatures and the elders the voice of many angels, numbering myriads of myriads and thousands of thousands, saying with a loud voice, "Worthy is the Lamb who was slain, to receive power and wealth and wisdom and might and honor and glory and blessing!" (Revelation 5:11-12)

QUESTIONS FOR COMMUNICATION AND APPLICATION

1. How can we more effectively fulfill the ministry of a priest to God with one another?

2. In what ways can we speak prophetically before the world to call them to righteousness and justice?

Adequate!

3. As you look at your relationships, do you see the commitment love and servant's lifestyle that communicate Christ to the world? How can you grow in this area?

Scripture Index

Adequate!

Adequate!

Adequate!

Leadership Resources
International

If you have been encouraged by this book, you might consider using it in a small group or class in your church. You might also consider inviting Bill to teach the Bible conference "God Uses Ordinary People" which is based on this book in your church.

Our desire is to magnify God in the eyes of His people so that they may stand in awe, wonder and worship before Him, and be transformed in His presence. We do this as we bring the encouragement of the Scriptures to churches, pastors and missions. The largest aspect of our work is encouraging and equipping pastors in the developing world who often have little formal training for the ministry. These ministries take place throughout Latin America, China, Burma, Russia and Africa. We invite your church to partner with us in one of these training times.

For more information about our conferences or materials, contact:

Leadership Resources
12575 South Ridgeland Avenue
Palos Heights, IL 60463
(800) 980–2226
www.leadershipresources.org